PMS is no laughing matter yet Mary manages to keep her humor intact while assuring women who have blown their top or sunk to the bottom of the emotional pit that there is hope. *S.O.S. for PMS* offers a well-reasoned and thoughtful approach to hormonal reality and is chock-full of advice-laden chapters. *S.O.S.* will be one of my most highly recommended books to friends and audiences. My ovaries and hormones salute you, Mary Byers, and so will those of other XX-chromosome readers!

JULIE BARNHILL, AUTHOR,
She's Gonna Blow; One Tough Mother; and
Motherhood, the Guilt That Keeps on Giving

Kudos to Mary Byers, who addresses PMS and the havoc it wreaks in families with truth and transparency. As a health professional, mother, wife, and PMS sufferer, I welcome Mary's approach and information. This book is packed with encouragement, practical advice and, perhaps most importantly, the affirmation that as women we are not alone and have a choice in how to respond to the chaos of PMS. Make the choice today to walk this journey with Mary as your guide.

KATHY PRIDE, RN, BSN
Author, *Winning the Drug War at Home*

Mary has done an excellent job in presenting helpful advice and recommendations on a very sensitive and confusing topic. Her book will help countless women at the mercy of PMS.

DR. ANGELIQUE RETTIG, MD
Fellow of American College of Obstetricians
and Gynecologists

Mary's use of a fictional character dealing with PMS, combined with the factual info, is a very captivating and effective tool. She provides a logical and systematic approach to treatment of an often very destructive problem for women and their families.

MONICA RAY, MD
nate of the Ameri<
of Famil

The
S.O.S.
for PMS

MARY M. BYERS

HARVEST HOUSE PUBLISHERS

EUGENE, OREGON

Published in association with the literary agency of Alive Communications, Inc., 7680 Goddard Street, Ste #200, Colorado Springs, CO 80920. www.alivecommunications.com.

Cover by Dugan Design Group, Bloomington, Minnesota

THE S.O.S FOR PMS
Copyright © 2008 by Mary M. Byers
Published by Harvest House Publishers
Eugene, Oregon 97402
www.harvesthousepublishers.com

Library of Congress Cataloging-in-Publication Data

Byers, Mary M.
The S.O.S for PMS / Mary M. Byers.
    p. cm.
    ISBN 978-0-7369-2170-1 (pbk.)
    1. Premenstrual syndrome—Popular works. I. Title.
    RG165.B94 2008
    618.1'72—dc22

                                 2008002348

Printed in the United States of America

08 09 10 11 12 13 14 15 16 / VP-SK / 11 10 9 8 7 6 5 4 3 2

*To every mom who has done or said something
she regrets while in the grip of PMS.
Tomorrow can be different than yesterday.*

*And to Catherine Price,
who has taught many to live courageously.*

Acknowledgments

I am grateful for the privilege to put words to paper and mindful of the team around me that makes it possible. I give special thanks to the following people.

My mom, Nancy Carlson: Since the beginning of my life you've encouraged me. Thank you for continuing to do so. Thanks also for being a proofreader extraordinaire, even if the task does turn you into the Comma Nazi!

The Harvest House team—LaRae Weikert, Carolyn McCready, Terry Glaspey, Betty Fletcher, Barb Gordon, Bob Hawkins, Jr., Christianne Debysingh, and the outstanding teams who support them: Not only are you excellent business partners, but I'm blessed to also call you friends.

Beth Jusino: It seems hard to believe we've done four books together already. Let's keep them coming!

My expert team: Dr. Bryan Albracht, Dr. Monica Ray, and Dr. Ron Eaker shared their medical expertise freely with me, and Drs. Albracht and Ray reviewed the medical chapters to ensure accuracy. I appreciate Dr. Angelique Rettig's interest in the topic and my personal situation. Two dieticians helped keep the accuracy of the nutritional information: Sara A. Lopinski, MS, RD, LDN, registered dietician, Center for Living at St. John's Hospital Prairie Heart Institute, and Amy D. Ozier, PhD, RD, LDN, CHES, assistant professor, School of Family, Consumer & Nutrition Sciences, Northern Illinois University. Thank you!

The focus group that birthed many of the ideas in this book: Julie, Dana, Tara, Libby.

The online survey respondents who answered my questions candidly and gave me permission to share with readers what I learned.

My Gal Pal team—Donna, Amy, Julie, Tara, Barb, and Pam: I love you all. Thanks for keeping me sane!

My home team—Stuart, Marissa, and Mason: You are my part-timers for life, and I wouldn't have it any other way. Thanks for loving me in spite of PMS and for supporting my work as a writer. I love you all more than you'll ever know.

My heavenly Father and His Son, Jesus, the author and perfecter of faith: My deepest desire is to be obedient to Your call on my life. Please give me ears to hear You and the courage to go wherever You ask me to.

Contents

My PMS Story

Irrational. Out of control. Angry. Crazed. These are just a few of the words women use to describe themselves when they are caught in the throes of Premenstrual Syndrome (PMS). I am one of those women, and this is my story. It may also be your story. You love your husband and children, but your struggle with PMS each month negatively impacts your relationships with them. Mothers "under the influence" (MUI) have done and said things they regret. We've lashed out at our children emotionally, verbally, and sometimes even physically. We're Dr. Jekylls and Mrs. Hydes. One minute we're cuddling our kids and the next we're screaming at them. PMS is not a pretty story, especially since we love our families and are often just as confounded by the mess we become each month as our mates and children are.

I was a freshman in college when I had my first out-of-control, mean-spirited, PMS rage. At the time I didn't realize it was attributable to PMS. I was as shocked by my outburst as my roommate, Catherine, was. After spewing a monologue of unfriendly and unkind words, I marched out of the room and went for a walk on campus, hoping to cool down, trying desperately to understand what had just happened. I remember where I was standing in our dorm room when I erupted. Thankfully, I don't remember the cutting words I spoke to her that day. Unfortunately, I do remember her response. While I was gone, she wrote me a note, apologizing for whatever she'd done to upset me. The truth was that she had done nothing at all. She was simply in the wrong place at the wrong time...as are so many family members when a PMS meltdown occurs. My outburst that day was fueled by the hormones in my body—the same ones that made it possible for me to eventually give birth to two children.

I've kept all the notes that Catherine and I exchanged our freshman year. They are a diary of our lives at Indiana University in Room 714 in the all-girls dorm. There are references to tough academic assignments, unrequited loves, disastrous dates, dashed hopes, and fulfilled dreams. The notes reflect the genuine love and appreciation we have for one another. Mostly they are funny, upbeat, and encouraging. Resting in the pile is also the note that should have alerted me to the problem that would affect my relationships throughout young adulthood, early marriage, and some of my mothering years.

Catherine's words speak to the confusion that many friends and family members feel when they've been scorched by a PMS tirade. Though her words were written years ago, they continue to haunt me for they capture a side of me I never wanted to admit existed. In part, Catherine wrote:

> Mary,
>
> …I can't figure out what's going on in your head at all…It was obvious that you were feeling angry about something this morning. I didn't know what…I really don't know where that anger you had came from. It just seemed to be there without anything setting it off. And I felt sort of victimized.
>
> …This is too unimportant in the scheme of things to let it put a wall between us and a riff in our friendship—which is a very precious thing to me. You mean far too much to me to have me let this go and not speak to you until who knows when.

Embarrassed by my tirade, I followed it by giving Catherine the silent treatment. Somehow I thought ignoring my infraction would erase its effects on our friendship. Catherine wasn't willing to ignore it, however, and I'm grateful that our relationship meant enough to her to address what happened. It's been more than 25 years since we lived together, and we're still in touch—an accomplishment I treasure.

Though my dorm-room explosion was the first angry eruption I can remember, it certainly wasn't the last. I managed to remain in denial for 15 years after I received Catherine's note. I ignored the outbursts that came like clockwork once a month. I overlooked the fact that during our early years of marriage my husband and I argued regularly once a month—approximately four weeks apart. I disregarded the cyclic, out-of-control tirades that colored my relationship with my precious stepson. I bristled at any suggestion that it was "that time of the month." I was insulted by suggestions that I was periodically oversensitive. In short, I refused to admit I had a problem. And since acknowledgment is the first step to healing, I continued to damage relationships, say things I'd later regret, and respond to others angrily rather than in love. Then two things happened:

- I gave birth to two children.
- My symptoms worsened.

The confluence of these two events made it unwise—and impossible—for me to continue to ignore the problem...unless I wanted to continue to be an unpredictable, out-of-control mother, which I did not. I had a decision to make: Do I have the courage to admit that I'm not always the person I want to be and that I need help to get through the toughest PMS days each month? Or do I continue to stick my head in the sand? Do I hope that—

- next month I'll be able to hold my breath and count to ten instead of succumbing to a hurtful outburst?
- my resolve to do "better" will finally kick in, making it possible for me to change the pattern...despite the fact I haven't been able to change it in the past?
- I'll eventually find a way to stop overreacting to tiny mothering irritations, which results in me putting my children in my crosshairs each month?

- I'll finally realize that it isn't appropriate to take my frustration and anger out on my husband every time PMS turns me inside out?

For many years I believed my PMS battle was unique. But as my children grew and I formed friendships with other mothers, I began to realize I wasn't alone. As I became more open about my battle with my hormones, other women began sharing their stories as well. Two things became clear: We all had incidents we were ashamed of, and, as mothers, we were concerned about how our lost battles to control PMS were affecting our children.

Though this book grew from my desire to understand what was happening to me monthly—and more importantly, what I could do about it—it quickly grew into a much bigger project. I held a focus group to listen to mothers talk about PMS firsthand. I conducted an online survey asking mothers to share their stories. I read a variety of books to better understand the causes and symptoms of PMS. I interviewed physicians and explored medical and alternative therapies. All this was done with one goal in mind: to help mothers—you and me—proactively manage PMS symptoms so that our families don't continue to bear the brunt of our unpredictable emotions month after month.

Plenty of books have been written about managing PMS. This is one of the few that address the challenge from a mother's point of view. If you've picked up this book, I suspect you too have experienced the debilitating effects of PMS and know how it reduces your ability to mother effectively. As you read, you'll discover ideas for making positive, proactive changes in your life that will ultimately bless your family as well.

Strengthening families by encouraging moms,

Mary Byers

1

There's Yellow Caution Tape in the Kitchen Again

Callie O'Keefe stood in the bathroom crying. Her two children, ages four and two, were outside the closed door, listening to their mother sob. Abby still felt the sting of her mother's hand on the back of her head. She'd made her younger sister cry, setting her mother off and resulting in the physical smack that seemed to come from nowhere with the speed of a rattlesnake strike. Abby stood in the hallway confused. Though she was the one who had been struck, her mother was the one crying.

As her children stood bewildered outside the bathroom door, Callie cried into a bathroom towel. "Lord, please help me stop this," she begged. "This is not the kind of mom I want to be!" This prayer had been uttered at least once a month for many years as she struggled with depression, anger, and fits of unpredictable behavior that descended on her prior to the onset of menstruation.

It was the same every month. The familiar twinge of oncoming cramps alerted her that her period would begin within the week, which meant she had to watch her words and actions very carefully. Each PMS battle started the same. Callie resolved to "do better and be kinder." And each resolution was quickly broken when her children set her off by arguing, complaining that the other got the bigger piece, or spilling a glass of milk at the very moment Callie's ability to cope was at its lowest. And it wasn't only the children who were bruised by her irrational behavior. Her husband, Steve, was just as likely to be the target of a tirade that she would later regret. Some nights it was so bad she'd wait until he was asleep and then slink into the guest room to bed down for the night. That way she wouldn't have to face him in the morning and see the hurt in his eyes.

As sobs racked her body, Callie grieved the fact that each month she seemed to get worse. What had started as mild PMS in her 20s was now cause for serious concern. Two children in the house and an inability to control her words and emotions was a combustible combination. Callie knew she was doing damage to the family and feared the long-term consequences.

She raised her head from the towel, looked into the mirror, and saw the face of a mother in agony. *Surely I'm not the only one who's out of control like this every month,* she decided. Callie remembered a neighbor down the street who had once mentioned at a party that her husband had nicknamed her "The Human Hurricane" because of the damage she did regularly while in the clutches of PMS. At the time Callie laughed because she couldn't imagine quiet, gentle Amber turning into anything close to a hurricane. But after the morning Callie just experienced, she now believed it was possible.

After rinsing her face with cool water, Callie opened the bathroom door and sat on the floor next to Abby. She gathered her sweet daughter into her lap, rested her chin on the top of Abby's head, and murmured the words she'd had to say so many times before: "Abby, mommy lost her temper, and she's very sorry. I was angry that you made Jessica cry, but how I handled it was inappropriate. I'm so sorry."

Abby's response was the same as always. "It's okay, Mommy. I love you." The ease with which she offered forgiveness amplified Callie's pain.

After hugging Jessica, Callie headed to the phone to make two calls. First, she'd call her physician to make an appointment to discuss her symptoms. Then she'd call Amber, the Human Hurricane, and ask if she'd come over some afternoon for a cup of coffee while the children napped. She finally realized she needed help and couldn't fight the PMS battle alone.

Though the phone calls were small steps, they would pay big dividends. By acknowledging the problem, Callie placed herself on the road to healing.

C allie is like me—and many women I know who suffer from severe PMS. We don't want to act the way we do. We're normally fairly balanced, kind people. We love our husbands and children. And yet, when triggered, we speak words we regret in an ugly tone of voice. We overreact. Sometimes we punish our children physically. Sometimes we rebuke them by ignoring them or withholding our love. One mother I interviewed confessed that, while under the influence of PMS, she ran away for a day when she felt she could no longer take the pressure of mothering.

Do you know you suffer from PMS? Or are you wondering if you do? Let's start by taking a closer look at the symptoms.

Physical Symptoms

- acne
- bloating, water retention, weight gain
- breast swelling and tenderness
- bruising
- changes in bowel habits (constipation/diarrhea)
- decreased sexual desire
- dizziness
- fatigue, lack of energy
- food cravings, especially for sweet or salty foods
- leg cramps
- nausea
- nipple discharge
- pain (headaches, aching muscles and joints, cramps, low back pain)
- rashes
- sensitivity to light
- shakiness
- sleep pattern changes and/or insomnia
- sweating
- swelling of hands and/or feet
- vaginal irritation

Behavioral and Emotional Symptoms

- anger
- anxiety
- decreased alertness
- depression, sadness, hopelessness
- forgetfulness
- inability to concentrate
- indecision
- irritability

- loneliness
- loss of control
- mood swings
- nightmares
- panic attacks

- paranoia
- suicidal thoughts
- unexplained crying
- withdrawal from family and friends

These are just a few of the 150 or so PMS symptoms that have been identified. Individually they are often manageable. When combined, they can be debilitating. According to WebMd:

- Although 85 percent of women experience PMS at times in their lives, about 40 percent are significantly affected.

- While most women first experience PMS in their mid-20s, PMS becomes even more common among women in their 30s.

- PMS can come and go during the reproductive years, and symptoms may worsen as a woman approaches perimeno-pause in the late 30s or 40s.

- Severe PMS symptoms may be premenstrual dysphoric dis-order (PMDD), which affects up to 8 percent of women.[1]

For the purpose of our discussions, I'll be dealing with PMS. How-ever, if you suffer from PMDD, please note: The symptoms you are wrestling with are more severe than regular PMS indications. Because of that, *it's even more essential that you be proactive in developing a personal coping plan.* The unexpected, unpredictable nature of PMDD mood swings, depression, and feelings of being overwhelmed make it extremely detrimental to mothering. The sooner you respond to the monthly tsunami that sweeps you away each month, the better off you and your family will be.

Mothers, be encouraged! You are not alone in the PMS battle, and you are not imagining your symptoms. Here's what a physician wrote about her own challenge each month:

When I asked my mother for help she could only offer sympathy. She told me that I'd probably grow out of it as I got older. Instead, it got worse. My PMS continued all through my medical training at Northwestern University in Chicago. One week out of the month I was in too much pain to do my work properly. I still remember the many afternoons when I had to leave the medical or pediatric ward. I went to the medical student on-call room and lay there in agony with severe nausea and cramps. My body swelled up so badly that I couldn't bear to bump against anything. The cysts in my breasts became large and tender. I was the only woman student on many of my rotations, and my symptoms made me feel inferior to and different from the male students. My moods fluctuated terribly. Part of the month I would feel calm and relaxed—like everyone else. But before my period I became quarrelsome and hard to deal with. I became much more sensitive to imagined or real slights and put-downs. I craved sugar and went on junk-food binges. Often I'd steal away and cry, not knowing how I was ever going to get through my training.[2]

Another physician wrote:

It is clear that PMS exists because among the thousands of women I have listened to, I have never had one say that each month, after her period, she loses self-esteem or fights with her husband or wants to kill herself. I have never heard a woman say that she wanted to feel postmenstrually as well as she does each month premenstrually. I've never heard a woman say, "You know, I get irritated easily, but premenstrually nothing could bother me."[3]

I'm sure you can identify with some of the symptoms and emotions just expressed. Though reviewing the list of symptoms in this chapter and realizing you have many (or all!) of them can be alarming, I hope you also experience relief and comfort. I remember hearing about PMS for the first time and thinking, *I have that!* I was so relieved to understand the cause for my wild mood swings and unpredictable behavior.

It's one thing to understand why questionable behavior is occurring. It's another to do something about it. In retrospect, that's where I dropped the ball. There were many reasons that my new awareness did not lead to behavioral changes. Mostly, I was not willing to admit to myself or anyone else that I was unable to control my emotions and the resulting actions. To do so would have required admitting a weakness, something I wasn't willing to do. (Then I became a mother. Suddenly all my weaknesses showed up, en masse, the minute I arrived home from the hospital with that bundle of pink blanket and joy in my arms!)

In addition to not wanting to admit my struggle, since I was married when my PMS worsened, it was much easier to blame my husband for my problems and expect him to be the one to change. Needless to say, that plan failed dismally.

It wasn't until I noticed that once a month my normally upbeat, positive nature melted into hopelessness, helplessness, and apathy that I begin to consider getting help. Honestly, the help wasn't so much for me as it was for my family. Month after month of irrational, uncontrollable, and unlike-me behavior finally took its toll. After struggling mightily to manage the unmanageable each month, I finally got down on my knees and admitted to God that I needed help. Then, like Callie, I called my doctor, acknowledged the problem to a friend (who, it turned out, had also been struggling alone with the problem), and admitted to my husband that "Black Tuesday" at our house was a result of my hormones—and not his shortcomings as a husband. (More on this later.)

My willingness to surrender was the turning point in my battle with PMS. By acknowledging it and being proactive, I've been able to lessen the effects on my family and me. Though I certainly haven't perfected my response, my family and I are more hopeful about it than we've ever been.

Skulking around, hoping PMS will go away on its own doesn't work. Admitting that there is a problem, enlisting help, searching for solutions that work, and making the changes necessary to minimize the effects of PMS are the only ways to slay the hormone dragon.

That's what this book is about: finding hope and taking back your life. Are you ready?

What If It's Not PMS, and This Is Just My Personality?

After Callie finished her calls and got the children down for their naps, she got out her journal. It was just a spiral notebook she'd picked up for a quarter during the back-to-school sales, but these days it seemed to be her lifeline. Though she didn't write every day, she did use the pages to capture her thoughts, clarify her thinking, and plan for the future. As she turned the pages to get to a blank one, an entry caught her eye:

> I'm depressed. I know I shouldn't be because blessings swirl around me, but I'm struggling with apathy, laziness, and lack of energy and clarity regarding what I should be focusing on right now. Where should my energy be going? Why can't I get excited about anything? Why am I apathetic toward my children? Toward Steve? I teeter between thinking I'm spoiled and selfish and wondering if I'm a bad mother because I feel like I'm sleepwalking through life these days. I'm unmotivated, unenergized, and feel like I'm wasting time. What is this all about?

The entry was dated one year ago. Abby had been three at the time and Jessica, one. Callie wondered if all mothers of young children felt this way or if it was just her. She continued to page through her diary until another entry grabbed her attention:

> I'm in a valley. I'm lethargic. Apathetic. Bored. I don't know how to pull myself out of this funk, and I'm worried about finding the

19

energy to meet my commitments over the next couple of weeks. Maybe I'm burned out. Maybe this is my mid-life crisis. Whatever it is, I don't like it. My family deserves better. But I don't know how to climb out of the valley. Lord, will You show me how?

Callie didn't remember writing the entry, but there it was on the page: her handwriting, her words, her plea for help. The entry was written on the fifteenth— exactly two months after the first entry that caught her eye. She turned a few more pages and read:

I am out of control. I screamed at the kids today for no real reason. Both started crying, and their crying made me even angrier. I put them down early for their naps because I couldn't stand having them around and didn't want to be a mother anymore. I envy my friends who don't have kids. They can do what they want, when they want, with whom they want. I can't.

What is wrong with me? Usually I love being a mother, but not today. Why am I so angry? Why do I hate my life? Why am I miserable? I wish I knew...

Though she put each outburst behind her and worked to forget the depression and lethargy she experienced each month, Callie could no longer ignore the evidence. She suffered from PMS, and it was affecting her most precious relationships. She took things out on her family members, and she knew it wasn't fair. She was ashamed of herself for doing so. She was glad she'd made an appointment with her doctor and pleased that Amber had agreed to stop by during nap time today. After seeing her struggle spelled out in ink in the pages of her journal, Callie decided she also needed to talk to Steve. She dreaded that conversation because she didn't like to admit she needed help. But the morning's events that led to her crying in the bathroom had unsettled her enough to convince her she couldn't battle her hormones alone. Now that she acknowledged what was causing her to lose herself each month, she had to do something about it. Her family deserved it. And, after reading her journal entries, she realized she needed to get a handle on her crankiness and depression for her own sake as well.

Callie is not alone in wondering about her behavior. During a focus group discussion, one of the women asked the question that became the title for this chapter: *What if it's not PMS, and this is just my personality?* According to the online survey I conducted for this book, other women have wondered the same thing. Though they suffer from PMS monthly and the symptoms are the same, many women are still surprised by the level of fury they feel—and the relief that floods them when their period starts and they think, "Oh, so *that's* why I was out of control."

Though Callie wondered if she was unique, she's actually not in this regard. PMS may worsen as a woman approaches perimenopause in her late 30s or 40s. Callie's journal entries reflect that this is true for her. In addition, her notes indicate a struggle with depression, which is not uncommon. Married women have higher rates of depression than unmarried women. Mothers of young children are very vulnerable to depressive symptoms, and the more children a woman has, the more likely it is that she'll become depressed.[1] Other factors that increase the likelihood of PMS are:

- significant emotional stress
- nutritional habits that contribute to PMS
- difficulty maintaining a stable weight
- lack of exercise[2]

Deep pain and regret accompany being a mother with PMS. Though childless women wrestle with the same symptoms, mothers often release their emotions and act out their frustration in front of their children. Here's what a few moms shared:

- My biggest regret is screaming and crying in front of my kids. A flood of emotion comes over me, and I just lose it. I talk out loud and cry to an audience of a six-year-old, four-year-old, and two-year-old as if they can solve my problem.

I just want someone to be in the pit with me because I feel so alone…What a sad picture to describe to you, and I really am embarrassed to admit it.

- My husband works Saturdays and we (the kids and I) catch up on cleaning before going out for fun. One Saturday there was just a lot of yelling (on my part) and crying (on their part). They ended up downstairs in front of the TV while I scrubbed the dining room floor with a small scrub brush on my hands and knees trying *very* hard to get out whatever was eating at me. I was afraid I was going to hurt my kids. Ultimately I had nothing to even be angry about.

- I know it's bad when at night I'm tucking the kids into bed and they pray that mommy won't be so crabby the next day.

- I lost my patience (and my mind) with my tired four-year-old who would not cooperate and get her pajamas on. I began screaming like a lunatic and forcing the pajamas over her head, giving her several smacks on the head out of sheer anger and frustration. It was awful…ugly and wrong.

- I make life hard on everyone around me. I'm not pleased by anything…After I had my first child, I was dealing with postpartum depression. I was getting into "PMS mode" when it hit me: *Life isn't worth this much pain. Why does this parenting thing have to be so hard? Wasn't having a baby bad enough?* Hundreds of those thoughts went through my head, so I did what I could to get my mind clear. I took a knife from the kitchen and started cutting my arms. It took the pain I had inside and made it less important than what was going on physically. For awhile it was as though I was numb. That was the only time I ever did that. It was there that God stepped in, and I knew I had to step out.

"God stepped in, and I knew I had to step out." That's really what this book is about: letting God step in to help us make changes that will lessen the effects of PMS on us and our families. It's almost like being in recovery. The first three steps of Alcoholics Anonymous speak to the power of surrender:

1. We admitted we were powerless over alcohol—that our lives had become unmanageable.
2. We came to believe that a Power greater than ourselves could restore us to sanity.
3. We made a decision to turn our will and our lives over to the care of God as we understood Him.

These three stages are applicable to PMS as well. It takes courage to admit that we need to make some changes in our lives. But as we acknowledge that our PMS is unmanageable and invite God into our process, we unleash His great power within us. By admitting that our lives have become unmanageable, and, more important, that God can restore us, we take the first important step to loosening the grip PMS has on us.

Because humans are creatures of habit, it's even harder to actually make the changes we desire. But here's something to ponder:

> If you always do what you've always done,
> you'll always get what you've always gotten.

If you continue to ignore the signs, be surprised by your outbursts each month, and regret your behavior after the fact, you'll continue to struggle until you reach menopause. But if you decide to make a determined effort to change your response to your symptoms from this day forward, you can write a different ending to your PMS story.

You're reading this book because you know or suspect you suffer from PMS. If you only read this book and make no life changes, our time together will be nothing more than a time of learning how other mothers deal with the problem. But if you read this book *and* implement the suggestions, our journey together will be a time of powerful transformation.

The good news is that we can lessen the effects of PMS on our lives. The even better news is that small changes pay big dividends. The bad news is that when we're Mothers Under the Influence (MUI) of PMS, it's hard to keep our emotions under control, our irritation in check, and hurtful words to ourselves. Because of this:

- We must decide we're ready to tackle PMS head-on.
- We must decide that next month will be different from last month.
- We must decide that we will be deliberate in determining which days of the month are the toughest for us and be proactive about developing a personalized coping plan.

All of this is possible to do, but it takes resolve and a firm commitment. We also have to be willing to admit to ourselves and to those closest to us that we suffer from PMS.

Major life transitions and changes occur at the moment of decision. When you decide that you're willing to do what it takes to change yourself and your patterns, healing begins. The moment of decision is also when God will step in and help. Do you want to make that decision right now? Don't wait for a defining moment like this mother experienced:

> My biggest regret would be denying [PMS] and making life miserable for everyone. I've only been suffering with PMS for the last few years—after the birth of my last child four years ago. I remember just last year screaming at the top of my lungs at my then three-year-old because she spilled her milk for the second time that day. The look on her face told me she was terrified. I'm supposed to be her safe haven. That's when I started to make changes.

It's hard to admit that you're not always the person or the mother you want to be. But once you admit it and identify specifically what you'd like to change, you've taken the first—and hardest—step.

Zeroing In

Are the physical symptoms of PMS what cause you the most trouble in your mothering? Or is it the behavioral and emotional symptoms that disrupt your caretaking? Most of the women I interviewed could usually handle the physical symptoms. According to these women cramps, headaches, bloating, food cravings, and fatigue are manageable. The emotional and behavioral symptoms are more difficult. Of those surveyed:

- 66 percent experience depression
- 76 percent struggle with anger
- 98 percent become irritable

In many cases, these symptoms produce the most disruption and cause the greatest damage in family life. Consequently, we'll spend more time discussing coping techniques for these issues in upcoming chapters than we will the physical symptoms of PMS. Why not take a minute and make a list of what bothers you the most and what changes you'd like to see. Your list might look like this:

What bothers me most	Changes I'd like to see
• how irritable I am and how I end up yelling	the ability to speak in a calm voice, even when I feel the internal turmoil
• how hopeless and depressed I feel	find a way to recognize my blessings in the midst of depression and minimize the sadness
• how overwhelmed I am each month	engage my family's help so that we're on the same team rather than working against each other
• how I treat my husband like an enemy	deal with my husband respectfully and lovingly

Your list will be as unique as you are. You don't have to share this list with anyone. It simply gives you goals for your new responses to PMS.

As we continue our journey together, consider this quote from Henry Ford: "Think you can or think you can't. Either way, you will be right." Think you can conquer PMS, and you will. Think you can't, and you won't. The choice is yours.

Have you decided to tackle PMS? Now that your mind is made up, read on to find out how to successfully adjust to life as a mother with PMS.

I'm Losing My Mind, and My Daughter Wants to Go to Target?

Amber arrived promptly at nap time, bearing blueberry muffins and a thermos of hot peach tea. Callie welcomed her but felt awkward. They had been neighbors for years, but only now was she reaching out. She was ashamed that it was because of her own need that she'd called her neighbor rather than a genuine desire to make a new friend. If Amber sensed it, however, she didn't let on.

"I'm so glad you called," Amber said as she followed Callie down the hall toward the kitchen. "Silence is the enemy of healing. I was quiet about my problems for far too long. I admire you for speaking up and reaching out."

"Thank you for coming," Callie responded. "I was afraid I might offend you by calling."

"You can't offend me. I'm an open book now. I believe in dealing honestly with problems rather than pretending I don't have any, which is what got me in trouble with Meg."

Callie remembered that Meg was Amber's oldest daughter. She'd heard through the grapevine that Meg had twice been through a residential treatment program for drug addiction.

"How is Meg?" Callie asked hesitantly.

"Doing wonderfully. Finally. I can't believe she survived her teenage years. Even more so, I can't believe her father and I did! But that's what ignoring problems does—makes them worse."

Callie felt strange having PMS compared to drug use, but she understood Amber's point: Ignoring a problem doesn't make it go away. She turned her attention back to Amber. "And how are your other two kids?" she asked with interest.

"Paul is a senior in college and is applying to grad school. I have no idea how we'll afford it, but he's a hard worker and will work part-time to help financially. Travis is a sophomore at the same college and seems to be more interested in playing his guitar than he is in passing chemistry. My husband says not to worry, that he'll get his act together eventually. I'm not so sure."

"Now that the kids are gone, what's keeping you busy?" Callie prompted.

"I've gone back to school, believe it or not. I got married before I graduated and never finished. I'm just 18 credits short of graduating. I've wanted to finish since the kids were little. David surprised me last Christmas with a gift certificate for tuition. I was hoping for a new piece of jewelry, and I get homework! Needless to say, I was less than thrilled. But the more I thought about it, the more excited I became. And it models the value of a degree for my kids. So far it's been grueling. But I'm enjoying being around young people and challenging my brain. Between that and caring for my mom, who has Alzheimer's, I'm keeping busy."

As the two women talked about caring for an aging parent, Callie relaxed and enjoyed Amber's company. Amber openly shared about changing her mother's diapers, putting in her dentures, and the agonizing decision to move her to a nursing home.

"She was madder than a hornet when we did it, but since she can't remember who I am, she can't bawl me out," Amber said and then laughed.

As the two women spoke, Callie saw how Amber's sense of humor helped her through the tough spots in her life. She wished she could develop her own sense of humor more fully. As a high-achieving firstborn, she was lacking in her ability to go with the flow, something she envied in Amber, even though they'd only been visiting a short time. Callie made a mental note to lighten up—and knew she'd have to work at it.

As Callie pondered her shortcomings, Amber suddenly changed the subject. "Enough about me. Let's talk about you!"

Callie felt exposed. Though she was enjoying this visit, she was hesitant to talk about the real reason Amber was in her kitchen. It was one thing to want help, but another to actually verbalize all that went wrong when PMS hit. Though Callie was grateful for Amber's company, right now she regretted calling her.

Amber interrupted her thoughts. "Let me guess. You don't want to tell me what happens when you have PMS because you can't bring yourself to admit what an ogre you become once a month. Am I right? You don't want to admit to being angry and overwhelmed. And you certainly don't want to admit that you're less than you want to be as a mother...and sometimes you're a jerk as a wife. Right?"

Callie stared at Amber, startled at her accuracy.

Amber continued. "Are there days when you feel like life isn't worth living anymore? When you feel like you're a terrible mother, your marriage is hopeless, and you just don't want to get out of bed?" She looked directly at Callie, measuring the response to her questions.

Callie struggled to find the words to confirm what Amber already knew.

Before she could speak, Amber placed her hand over hers, softened her voice and said, "It's okay, Callie. I've been there. I almost lost my marriage over it, and my estrangement from Meg started because my PMS was at its worst when she was rebelling so terribly. In fact, I remember one horrible day when I stood bawling in the kitchen in reaction to a remark Meg made. I was in such deep pain and so overwhelmed. I tried to explain to her what I was feeling. Like most teens though, she was self-absorbed. I remember struggling to make my pain real to her. When I was done she simply said, 'Oh. By the way, can we go to Target?' I remember thinking, *I'm losing my mind, and my daughter wants to go to Target?* It was like an out-of-body experience.

"I wish I'd faced the obvious about how my hormones were affecting me and my family. But no one talked about it back then. I suffered in silence. I don't want you to do the same. Silence is the enemy of healing. I'm here to listen and here to help."

Amber's understanding and compassion were too much for Callie. She began to cry. Once the tears came, they wouldn't stop. She tried hard to still her sobs, but they sprang forth in a torrent. Amber opened her purse and offered a packet of tissues, sitting silently while Callie mourned what her life had become.

Are you like Callie—afraid to appear weak by admitting you struggle with PMS? I was—until I discovered that many of my friends were also suffering in silence. Our conversations often started with a joke about PMS as we gingerly gauged whether we shared the same struggles. But when we discovered we were mutual "hormone hostages," the conversations quickly moved from lighthearted joking to the deep pain associated with being an out-of-control mother and spouse once a month. Realizing I wasn't alone made me hopeful that I could learn to manage the mood swings and meltdowns that colored my days. Perhaps knowing you're part of a broader sisterhood will help you as well.

In his book *Holy Hormones,* Dr. Ron Eaker writes, "PMS is real! It is a medical entity that is defined by a spectrum of symptoms that can be both physical and emotional. It may intensify in the early to mid-forties and is sometimes confused with perimenopausal changes."[1] I was relieved to hear a physician recognize and acknowledge PMS as a reality. Sometimes I wondered if I were imagining things, even though the PMS grip held me so tightly in its clutches.

One of the most frequent questions Dr. Eaker hears from women in his practice is, "Am I going crazy?" You may have wondered this too.

You are not going crazy and neither am I! But we *will* go crazy if we don't decide to proactively manage our PMS rather than wistfully hoping it will go away on its own. Here's a scary thought: Because symptoms may worsen as you approach perimenopause in your late 30s or 40s, your symptoms might be at their worst when your children are in their teens, depending on their current ages. Children cause stress. Stress magnifies PMS. Therefore, your children may, in fact, be heightening your PMS response each month. (We'll discuss this more later.)

I've heard many mothers hesitantly assert, "My PMS seems to be getting worse." That's because as we age and approach perimenopause, it often *is* getting worse. It's not just "all in your head." After menopause, many of the challenges you're experiencing now will lessen or go away altogether. But for many of us, our kids may well have left the nest by the time our symptoms dissipate. That's why we need to get things under control now.

Whether you have a mild case of PMS each month or a severe case, it's essential to get serious about minimizing the effects on you and your family. Children often are the innocent victims of PMS rage and unpredictable hormonal behavior. One minute you're quietly working in the kitchen, and the next minute you're in the family room waving around a dish towel and yelling.

Has this happened to you? It has to me. The change from quiet to out-of-control was almost as confusing and frightening for me as it was for my kids.

After a tirade, how do you respond? Do you cry? Pretend it didn't happen? Give your offspring the cold shoulder when they try to understand what set you off?

Though our symptoms may be similar, we're all different in regard to the severity, length, and number of effects we experience. We're also different in our ability to respond to them. That's the challenge in understanding PMS. All women are unique, so our combination of symptoms and the way we respond to them is also unique. What bothers you may not bother me. What causes me to have a meltdown might roll off your back. In a PMS focus group I asked women what troubled them most about PMS. Here are their answers:

- less engagement and interest in people and activities
- anger
- less tolerance
- feeling out of control
- knowing I'm irrational but not being able to stop myself
- inability to summon the love for my family that's usually present in abundance but missing when I have PMS
- saying things I wouldn't normally say

Can you identify with any of those answers? What bothers you most about your PMS?

Because symptoms and coping mechanisms differ among women, responding to PMS requires a personalized approach. Over the next couple of chapters, we'll look at the variety of factors that influence PMS and how to get a handle on them. Some of these may directly affect you and some may not. I invite you to take notes in the margins or highlight the issues you want to consider further.

One thing is for sure. Because PMS is a multilayered challenge, our response needs to be multilayered as well. Your personal solution to minimizing the effects may include a combination of coping techniques, physical activity, changes in diet and sleep habits, and possibly medication or natural supplements. (Though I haven't been able to implement this yet, my personal plan includes a hammock, a good book, and a monthly trip to a deserted island.) Only you can fully know what's best for you and your body.

Before you read on, let's take a cue from Amber, whose humor helps her through difficult situations. I don't know who compiled this list, but it's great.

Eleven Things PMS Stands For

1. Pass my sweatpants
2. Psychotic mood shift
3. Perpetual munching spree
4. Puffy mid-section
5. People make me sick
6. Provide me with sweets
7. Pardon my sobbing
8. Pimples may surface
9. Pass my shotgun
10. Pack my stuff
11. Potential murder suspect

Occasionally, when I'm deep in the throes of nasty PMS, I'll go to my computer and reread this list. I get a kick out of seeing myself in these descriptions—even the last one. As a Christian, I'm uncomfortable thinking about murder, but as a PMS mom, I know how intense emotions can be. I figure that as long as I focus on keeping the "potential" in "murder suspect," it's okay for me to laugh at these tongue-in-cheek insights. Feel free to add your own definitions to the list.

Charting Your Course and Navigating the Whitewater

For the first time ever, Callie was acknowledging the truth. She confided to Amber, "I'm a monster when I have PMS. Sometimes I don't want to get out of bed. Sometimes I can barely function. I usually end up yelling at the kids and sometimes worse. And frankly, once a month I think I made a mistake and should have married someone else. I go from being independent and capable one day to being despondent and overwhelmed the next. I just don't get it."

"I'm not sure there's anything to get," Amber remarked. "The key is to learn to manage what comes your way every month."

"Were you able to do that?"

"It took a while and I'm not perfect, but it sure is better than letting myself be surprised and overwhelmed every month."

"How did you do it?"

"Acknowledging I had a problem was the first step. Initially I was only willing to admit it to myself. Then finally I confided in David."

"How did he respond?"

"Honestly? He wondered what took me so long to make the connection between my hormones and my behavior! I was furious at him for even making the suggestion that there was a connection. But when he gently pointed out that we generally fought at least once a month, at approximately the same time each month, I started to realize how my cycle was affecting him as well. As we talked, he even confessed he had a secret code on his calendar at work so that he could track when I was most likely to be grumpy. I was mortified. But that conversation was sobering, and I realized I could no longer pretend I didn't have a problem."

"So let me guess," said Callie. "You waved a magic wand or took a magic pill and all the problems went away. Right?"

"Wrong. Managing PMS isn't nearly that simple. I wish it were. It takes commitment and perseverance to conquer it. But it's worth it."

"What's the secret?"

"First, as I said, you have to acknowledge it. You've done that. Then you have to chart it. When you know it's coming, it's easier to handle." Amber sat back in her chair.

"Chart it? What do you mean?"

"Simple. I kept a calendar for several months," Amber shared. "I used different colors of markers to record the severity of my symptoms. Unbelievably, a distinct pattern emerged—so specific that I could predict what days I would feel the worst, what days I would feel overwhelmed, what days I was more likely to snap at family members, and what days David needed to take us out to dinner when he got home from work."

"Are you kidding?"

"No! I'm dead serious. The worst day of the month became known as 'Mad Monday' at our house. On that day, David would try to get home from work earlier than usual. I'd have the kids ready to go, and we'd climb into the car and head out to dinner. Or sometimes he'd bring something home with him and feed the kids while I crawled into a hot bath. I hated being that needy, but I have to tell you, it was wonderful to be cared for like that."

Callie looked at Amber in disbelief. She didn't know what she'd expected to hear, but it certainly wasn't this. She thought perhaps she'd learn about some amazing medicine she could take or a form of home therapy she could use. But charting her symptoms? Mad Monday? These ideas seemed too simple to be effective.

Callie pressed Amber further, determined to find a coping technique that was more advanced, medical, or scientific. "Then what?" she asked.

"After I discovered the pattern, I adjusted my schedule accordingly. I started going to bed earlier a few days before I knew the tsunami would hit. I made sure I got up before the kids and walked on the days that would be the worst, and I watched my intake of caffeine and alcohol. I did other things too, such as planning activities for the kids that would keep them busy and out of my hair.

Sometimes we'd go to the park, or the McDonald's Playland, or the library. Or I'd let them play on the computer a little extra on the tough days. Anything to keep me from flying off the handle with them. I know that sounds wimpy, but desperate times make desperate mothers."

"That's for sure!" Callie agreed, but she was disappointed in what she was hearing. It seemed so regular, so every day. She'd hoped for something more.

Amber sensed her hesitation. "Callie, would you do me and your family a favor? Would you just try it? I know it sounds simple, but there's a powerful principle behind charting your emotions and behavior: *That which is predictable is also preventable.* I learned this from the counselor I was seeing to help with Meg's problems. There's a lot of truth to it. To respond effectively to the wild monthly mood swings you're having, you have to know when they're coming. When you do, you can more ably prevent them from getting out of control."

"I'll try it," Callie finally agreed. "But I'm skeptical."

"Would you feel better if what I suggested was more difficult or required more effort on your part?"

"I suppose so."

"Charting your experience is easy, Callie. The hard part comes when it's time to respond to what you've learned. But if you're willing to do it, I can almost promise that your life will be different. Knowledge is power. Knowing what to expect each month gives you the power to hedge against it. Take this seriously, Callie. Doing so will help you get through this better than I did. I seriously jeopardized relationships before I figured out what to do. I don't want you to go through that."

"Relationships certainly are important to me, Amber. Since you swear by it, I'll try it."

"Atta girl! Why don't we get together next month to see where you're at? I'll bring the treats again, and you bring your chart. Okay?"

Callie laughed and shook her head. "I feel silly about this, Amber. But those muffins were awfully good. If that's what it takes to get a second batch from you, I'm up for it!"

There is power in acknowledging you have PMS. Admitting it to another person is difficult, but letting the secret out also brings relief and hope. By agreeing to chart her monthly moods, Callie took the first step in sending an S.O.S. for her PMS.

Though I know I struggle with PMS and should be on the lookout for it each month, I'm still occasionally surprised by the stealth of its arrival, the fury that overtakes me, and the wake of destruction it leaves in its path. After a 20-year struggle (worse in the last decade), you'd think I'd have a firm grip. But repeatedly I'm caught unaware and am paralyzed by what I see happening to myself—unless I stay focused on my monthly chart.

Therein lies part of the problem. I'm so busy being a wife, mother, and entrepreneur that I neglect watching for what's ahead each month. I know you're busy too. And that may be our biggest problem. Though PMS is foreseeable, repetitive, and predictable, it manages to sneak up on us over and over simply because we're busy and not paying attention to our menstrual cycle. In addition, some of us find it hard to believe that understanding our cycle can make a huge difference. Here's how some moms are using their knowledge to help them cope with PMS.

- I try to get more rest the day or two before my "friend" starts.
- I talk to/warn my husband and try not to make any major decisions.
- I schedule more "me" time.
- I avoid caffeine, sugar, MSG, and sodium during the last 16 to 18 days of my cycle.
- I lighten my load if possible.
- I try to get to bed earlier or take a 20-minute nap while the kids are napping.
- I try to schedule less and keep life simple.
- I tell my husband about it…then I take a bubble bath and

watch TV in bed alone for a while. A good night's sleep does wonders to restore my head and perspective.

- I tell the kids that mommy needs a timeout. I go in my room, shut my door, and get into bed for a couple of minutes. If I allow myself those two minutes, I can take a deep breath and bring things back into perspective. If I don't take that little bit of time alone, things keep building until I blow.

- I exercise, eat better, and pray.

- I drink lots of water.

- I try to stay quiet and take regular breaks.

- I constantly remind myself that I will feel better next week.

- I try not to push myself to do all my chores.

To be able to use any (or all) of these coping mechanisms, we must recognize where we are in our cycle and what to expect as a result. That's why it's so important to chart our symptoms for *two to three months*. We need to identify our personal premenstrual patterns.

When I finally acknowledged I had a serious problem with PMS, I began making notations on my calendar, identifying the worst days with a red star. It was a crude way to track my symptoms, but it soon made it possible for me to know when to expect the darkest, out-of-control days. For a while those days occurred consistently on Tuesdays, which became known at my house as "Black Tuesdays." The phrase became a code between my husband and me. All I had to do was say these two words and his attitude toward me would soften. I suspect he gave me a wide berth at that time as well, although I never noticed it in a negative way. (You can read my husband's perspective later in this book.)

There's another important benefit to tracking your symptoms: You can provide specific, detailed information to your doctor. Handing a completed symptom chart to your physician makes it much easier for him or her to help you in constructive ways. Dr. Ron Eaker notes,

"I have had many women come to the office complaining of various problems that lead me to suspect PMS may be the source. Without the qualification and documentation of the symptoms, I often have to delay any treatment plan until I can verify my hunches. The symptom diary does this most effectively."[1]

I've included two types of symptom trackers at the end of this chapter. One is simply a blank calendar outline. I've provided for two months to make it easier for you. You may photocopy them, fill in the appropriate dates for each month you plan to track your cycle, and then simply note which days are the roughest for you. It's most helpful if you record actual symptoms (see chapter 1 for a list) so you can identify which bother you early in your cycle and which are worse immediately prior to the onset of menstruation. Though this is a simplified method of tracking symptoms, it's still very effective. After several months, you'll likely see patterns that will be helpful in planning your PMS activity level and responses. (Most experts suggest tracking your symptoms for a minimum of three months. This allows for month-to-month variation and enables you to more easily see your pattern.)

The second tracking chart allows you to easily make a month-to-month comparison regarding your symptoms. As you'll see, each column represents a month, and each row represents a day of the month. You record your symptoms the day they occur, along with the beginning and end of menstruation. (In the next chapter, we'll review a completed sample to see what we can learn from this information.)

I personally found it easiest to leave a paper copy of my chart on my headboard or the kitchen counter. Then, while cooking dinner or at the end of the day, I could record my emotions and behaviors without having to log onto my computer.

It doesn't matter which chart you use. What is important is that you invest the time and energy into charting your symptoms each month. When you have the results of two or three months of record keeping, you'll be able to determine when your own "Mad Monday,"

"Black Tuesday," or "Ferocious Friday" will occur. Further, you can alert your loved ones, adjust your schedule as necessary, and easily communicate with your physician should you wish to consult him or her. Charting takes just seconds a day, but it pays big dividends. It's easy, it's free, and there are no side effects. If you're serious about reducing the collateral damage of PMS in your home, it's an essential step. I hope you'll start today!

Month_____

PMS Symptoms

Sun	Mon	Tue	Wed	Thu	Fri	Sat

Month _____

PMS Symptoms

Sun	Mon	Tue	Wed	Thu	Fri	Sat

PMS Symptoms

	January	February	March	April	May	June	July	August	September	October	November	December
1												
2												
3												
4												
5												
6												
7												
8												
9												
10												
11												
12												
13												
14												
15												

16															
17															
18															
19															
20															
21															
22															
23															
24															
25															
26															
27															
28															
29															
30															
31															

PMS Basics

Callie stood in the rain on Amber's doorstep clutching her calendar. It was Veteran's Day, and Steve was home with the kids. After a terrible weekend fraught with PMS tension, he'd volunteered to watch the kids while she got out of the house. She eagerly accepted his invitation but had no idea where she wanted to go. Out of the blue, Amber called to schedule a follow-up visit. When she learned Callie was free, she suggested meeting at her house today. Callie considered it divine intervention.

Amber answered the door, and Callie stepped inside. The warmth enveloped her as she closed her umbrella and removed her coat. Callie smelled cinnamon in the air while simultaneously noting Amber's new haircut.

"Your hair is darling!" Callie exclaimed.

"Thanks. Hanging around with students has made me realize how 'old' I've become in my thoughts and actions. Some of them change their cut—and color—as often as once a week. I've had the same haircut since my first child was born. I decided it was time for a change."

"I love it! What did David think?"

"He did a double-take when he walked in the day I got it cut. Then he swept me in his arms and planted a smooch on my lips, something he usually doesn't do. I decided right then and there that I needed to update more of myself. Slowly I've been getting rid of the clothes I've had for centuries. I had a makeup lesson at the mall. I bought new pajamas, got rid of the hiking boots I've had since college, and I started walking every morning before I leave to visit my mom. I feel great."

Callie envied Amber, but only for a second. She was glad something as simple as a haircut could lead to so many positive changes. She wondered if she should get her hair cut too.

"Come on!" Amber gestured as she turned to walk down the hall. "There are pumpkin muffins and tea in the Florida room. We can watch it rain while we talk."

"Raining on the inside is how I've felt the past several days, Amber. I'm so glad you invited me over. I didn't think I could take one more minute of mothering. Not only did you save me, you saved my kids and husband as well!" Callie giggled.

Amber gave her a knowing look. "The library used to be my refuge on days like today. I'd let my kids pick out a stack of books, and we'd settle in the children's area. If I was lucky, the current issue of *People* magazine would be in and I could lose myself in other people's lives for a short time. If I wasn't lucky, Meg would insist that I read a book to her. It was such an innocent request— one I usually loved—but it was so hard to do when I had PMS. I missed a lot of opportunities for bonding with my kids when they were young. Sometimes the memories make me sad."

Callie felt the weight of Amber's words. She was often sad too. It seemed so unfair...to love so deeply but be incapacitated for days at a time. She studied Amber's face and wondered if she'd be able to control her PMS sooner rather than later so she wouldn't have the same level of regret. She hoped so.

"Would it make any difference if you knew your struggle has already helped me immensely?" Callie offered. "Just talking about it with another woman lessened some of my angst and gave me hope that coping mechanisms that will help are out there."

Amber looked up from her reverie and smiled. "I'm glad. I'd love to see you free from the grip of PMS."

"I'm in its grip right now. When I felt it coming, I crossed a couple of things off my To-Do list and took a nap with the kids on Saturday. Yesterday I asked Steve to watch the kids so I could go to the grocery store by myself. Today I get to be here with you. I'm feeling more focused and centered than I have in a long time. I think you're rubbing off on me!" Callie smiled and then asked about Amber's classes.

"I'm doing well," she replied. "My classmates tease me about setting the grading curve high, but going to school is different at my age. I don't have as many distractions as they do, I'm not working like many of them are, and I have a strong desire to excel that I didn't have when I was younger. It's been fun."

"What's your favorite class?"

"Art history, believe it or not. It's a lot of memorization, so it's difficult. But I love studying the paintings and learning who painted them, who their artistic influences were, and what era they painted in. The knowledge probably is useless, but I'm fascinated. If nothing else, I should be able to answer a Trivial Pursuit question or two when the kids come home for Christmas."

"How's your mom?" Callie inquired as Amber stopped to pour tea.

"Not good, Callie. She's failing fast. It's so hard to watch, but she hasn't been herself for a long time. I don't know if it's worse losing a parent quickly and unexpectedly or watching this slow descent. At least this way I have time to prepare for losing her, although the truth is we lost the mom we knew a long time ago when her mind started to go. She doesn't recognize me, and she's often physically abusive. Caring for her is the hardest thing I've ever done."

Suddenly Callie felt silly sitting in Amber's house with her color-coded calendar. Her problems seemed so minute compared to Amber's. And yet she couldn't dismiss the awful truth hiding behind her front door: For several days of the month she was irrational, unfair, unkind, unwilling, and uninterested. This wasn't the kind of person she wanted to be.

Callie placed her calendar on the table and explained, "The days marked with an 'M' are days I menstruated. The days shaded yellow represent bright and sunny moods. The green days represent days I was edgy and irritable. The black days were the worst."

Amber noticed there were five days blacked out.

Callie looked at Amber, waiting for her response.

"This is a good start, Callie," she replied. "Was it helpful to you?"

"Yes and no. Poor Steve! Even though I could tell by the chart that my edginess and irritation was due to PMS, I couldn't stop myself from overreacting. I caught myself being short-tempered with him. I was quick to apologize, however, and when I realized what was happening, I took a walk around the block. I think the more I focus on finding solutions for the bad days, the better it will be in the long run. I can see that I'm going to have to remain committed for the long haul."

Callie discovered the same thing I've learned: There's no quick fix for the symptoms of PMS. But the more knowledgeable we are about what's happening to our bodies and the more we focus on proactively responding to what we know, the more likely we are to be successful in managing PMS in a positive way.

Since writing a book takes me months, it was inevitable that I would have my own "black days" on this project. In fact, ironically, I had such a day when I started working on this manuscript. What a grim reminder of how incapacitating PMS can be! At first I welcomed my descent into the depths of PMS. I figured it would be good fodder for my writing and enable me to share from a heartfelt, on-the-spot experience. There was only one problem: I didn't have the motivation to write about it when I was a Mother Under the Influence. Instead I stared blankly at my computer screen while wrestling with sadness, despair, depression, doubt, listlessness, and apathy. With the cloud of PMS hanging over my head, I wondered how I could possibly find the energy and enthusiasm to string together 56,000 words in a way that would encourage and uplift other moms struggling with the same emotions. I berated myself because I procrastinated. I made long mental lists of all the reasons I'm not a good mom. And instead of writing, I stared at the growing pile of laundry and prayed for a fairy godmother to show up and make life disappear. Then I took a bath.

My friend Tara e-mailed me during this time to ask how the book was coming. I confessed to being in the grips of PMS and told her I was having difficulty finding the motivation to write. She was surprised that experiencing it didn't make it easier to capture it on the page. Then, a month later, she wrote:

> I have PMS right now and have decided that if you wrote your book while having PMS it would read something like: "I HATE PMS. IT MAKES ME NUTS. IT MAKES MY FAMILY NUTS. I HATE NUTS TOO—ALL KINDS:

PECANS, WALNUTS, EVEN THOSE BLASTED
MACADAMIAS FROM HAWAII. HECK, I HATE
THIS BOOK TOO. I'M GOING TO GO TO BED
AND EAT CHOCOLATE.

I chuckled when I read her note. And now, when I think of PMS, I can't help but think of *nuts*—all kinds of them.

Thankfully, a week later my symptoms disappeared. My energy and enthusiasm returned, and I'm more determined than ever to make it possible for you to minimize the effects of PMS on your life and the lives of your family.

Hopefully, the charting exercise in the last chapter will give you valuable information about your cycle. I chose to present that material first so you can quickly and proactively take a step toward solving the PMS puzzle in your life. Now, let's take a step back and understand a little of what's happening to us physically each month so we can better prepare for it.

The Physiology

I researched PMS in-depth before I started writing. Some of the medical research was well over my head. I didn't really want to understand *everything* that's happening to my body every month—I simply wanted enough knowledge to help me create a workable solution that would keep me from flying off the handle and damaging my relationships. I was mindful of this as I conducted my research. Consequently, I'm presenting a simplified overview in this chapter of what's really a complex process. This general understanding will be beneficial to you as you develop your personalized coping plan. If you want to know more, there are plenty of resources available.

In their book *PMS: Women Tell Women How to Control Premenstrual Syndrome,* Stephanie DeGraff Bender and Kathleen Kelleher quote an article from the *American Journal of Psychiatry* that describes premenstrual syndrome as a "menstrually related physical/ psychological disorder that can be defined as 'the cyclic occurrence of symptoms that are of sufficient severity to interfere with some aspects of life, and which appear with a consistent and predictable relationship to menses.'"[1] Further, these authors write, "At the beginning of their definitive article on PMS, in the *American Journal of Obstetrics and Gynecology,* Drs. Reid and Yen state that a temporary deterioration in a woman's interpersonal relationships frequently develops in the premenstrual week."[2]

I was in an airport when I read that last sentence, and I had to stifle a laugh as I read the words "temporary deterioration." *It's a deterioration, all right!* Behind my laughter was much pain. I suspect you share it as well—the pain of angry words, missed opportunities, love withheld, and unrelenting self-flagellation. The monthly "temporary deterioration" leaves us saddened, exhausted, regretful, and full of self-loathing. And that's just our response to our actions. It doesn't take into consideration the angry and hurt feelings we leave and encounter in our path.

Changes in our bodies each month result in our radical behavior. It's helpful to understand these changes, even if only on a surface level, in order to more fully understand why we can be pleasant one moment and raging the next. There are four phases to the menstrual cycle, which averages 28 days. The following information is from Lori Futterman and John Jones' book *PMS, Perimenopause, and You.*

Phase of Cycle	Follicular	Ovulatory	Luteal	Menstrual
Average Days	12 to 13	2	8 to 11	3 to 5

Follicular Phase: The hypothalamus–pituitary complex generates a hormone called *follicle stimulating hormone* (FSH). This substance stimulates cells within the ovaries, called follicles, to produce estrogen. Once the estrogen level has risen to a sufficient amount, all but one of these follicles shrink, leaving the remaining one to become an egg.

Ovulatory Phase: This surviving follicle enlarges and ruptures under the stimulation of the pituitary's *luteinizing hormone (LH).* This hormone also stimulates the production of testosterone, which peaks during this phase. The egg then develops into the corpus luteum, which releases progesterone. During this phase, the egg breaks loose to enter the fallopian tube, which can cause a feeling of pain termed *mittelschmerz.* [I love the word *mittelschmerz!* It's German and literally means "middle pain," which refers to the pain midway between menstrual periods. I'm going to start using it when I have PMS and lose my temper. Perhaps the fun of saying the word will lighten my mood. I can see it now: The next time someone spills a glass of milk when I have PMS, I'll respond by saying, "Oh, Mittelschmerz!"]

Luteal Phase: This phase is dominated by another hormone produced by the ovaries—progesterone. When the progesterone level peaks, estrogen rises again from its low level during the ovulatory phase. Both then begin to decline. Progesterone helps the body to sustain and nourish pregnancy. During this phase, testosterone probably decreases as well. By this time, your body has prepared itself for pregnancy.

Menstrual Phase: The rapid loss of progesterone triggers the bleeding that signals the beginning of the menstrual phase. Both progesterone and estrogen reach their lowest points during this phase.[3]

The luteal phase of your cycle (the second half, prior to menstruation) is when PMS symptoms generally occur. When you have charted yourself, you should be able to predict with accuracy when your toughest days of the month will be.

If you want to specifically pinpoint when your luteal phase will begin, it helps to determine when you will ovulate, which is "usually the halfway point in your cycle. If you have a 28-day cycle, the halfway point is from the 13th to 15th days. You can tell when you ovulate because you will feel a little bit of cramping or pain in your lower abdomen, and your vaginal discharge will be heavier and have more mucus."[4] Once you identify ovulation, it's easier to identify the luteal phase (or what I call the "Let's just all go get on the Titanic" phase). Then you can proactively employ the coping techniques we'll be exploring.

Though medical researchers do not agree on the exact cause of PMS, they do agree that it is physical in nature. According to DeGraff Bender and Kelleher, "Most believe that PMS is a hormonally based disorder that is the result of changes in the levels of one or two female sex hormones—progesterone and estrogen. It may be either a low level of progesterone or a ratio imbalance between progesterone and estrogen. The most widely accepted theory is that a deficiency in progesterone occurs during the luteal phase of the menstrual cycle (the time between ovulation and menstruation)."[5]

Note that it's possible for you to have PMS symptoms even if you're not menstruating. Women who have had a partial hysterectomy (the uterus is removed, but the ovaries are left intact), who are heavily involved in sports and not menstruating as a result, who are anorexic and not having a period, who are nursing, or who are going through perimenopause and having erratic periods all may still have PMS even though they aren't having a traditional or regular cycle.

Obviously, seeing patterns will be much more difficult if you don't have a regular menstrual cycle and can't compare charts from month to month. Yet there is still a benefit to seeing your rhythms recorded on paper. Recording your emotions forces you to notice how you're feeling. To know more about your personal PMS symptoms and how they affect you, notice when they come, notice how you feel, and notice how you react. When you observe these things about yourself, whether you have a regular cycle or not, you'll be able to respond to your hormonal changes rather than being caught off guard and reacting.

As you're working on identifying and charting your symptoms, it's interesting to compare how you stack up to women who have been diagnosed as having PMS after charting their menstrual cycles for at least two months. Of 1,079 self-reports filled out by women:

- 57 percent reported that they were not the only ones to notice their symptoms.
- 83 percent reported that symptoms increased as they got older.
- 98 percent reported "loss of control" as the most problematic issue.
- 56 percent reported that their symptoms ended gradually each month, while 36 percent indicated that symptoms ended quickly with the onset of menstruation.
- 99 percent described themselves as more energetic and more positive in their outlook on life following their menstrual period.
- 79 percent reported that they had been verbally abusive toward other people when they were premenstrual.
- 29 percent reported they had been physically abusive when they were premenstrual.
- 85 percent reported that their symptoms negatively affected their job performance.[6]

Now, let's look at a set of charts for "Laura" to see how we can use the information recorded to develop a plan. As you look at the sample chart comparing three months, watch for patterns. This will be valuable practice for interpreting your own chart when you've completed three consecutive months of charting.

Laura's Chart

	January	February	March	April	May	June	July	August	September	October	November	December
1												
2												
3												
4												
5												
6												
7												
8												
9												
10												
11												
12		F, S										
13		F, I, S										
14		S	S									
15		S	S									
16		I, ST	S									

	17	B, I, ST, IN	S, ST					
	18	B, I, ST, IN	B, S					
	19	B, I, ST, IN	(B), I, ST, IN					
	20	I, ST	(B), I, ST, IN					
	21	BA	B, I, ST, IN					
	22	M	B, I, ST, IN					
	23	M	I, ST					
M	24	M						
M	25	M						
M	26	M						
M	27	M						
M	28	M						
M	29	M						
	30							
	31							

B = Bloating   I = Irritability   ST = Stress   BA = Backache

F = Fatigue   S = Sadness   IN = Indecisiveness

See chapter 1 for a complete list of symptoms. Use the symptoms most relevant to you when you complete your chart. To indicate severe symptoms, place a circle around the symptom initial (see February 16).

Interpreting the Chart

After you've charted yourself for several months, you'll want to make observations that will help you manage your PMS. Take a quick look at Laura's chart. There are several things noticeable right away:

- Laura has periods that last five to six days, depending on the month (indicated by the letter "M").

- The symptoms that bother her most are bloating, fatigue, irritability, sadness, stress, and indecisiveness. Though other symptoms may bother her, they aren't severe enough for her to record them on the chart.

- Fatigue is a problem about 1-1/2 weeks before her period. This is helpful for her to know for scheduling purposes.

- She's most stressed and irritable immediately before her period. Knowing this, she can identify which days are likely to be her most difficult before they happen, allowing her to schedule carefully during this time and perhaps rely more on her husband for help with their children.

- Because she's indecisive in the days leading up to her period, she can avoid making major decisions at that time or ask for help from her husband or a trusted friend when necessary.

- Her symptoms disappear with the onset of menstruation, with the exception of a backache that sometimes occurs on the first day. Knowing this, she may plan to be less active the week before her period but fully active during her period.

These six observations give Laura power. First, she knows her menstrual cycle usually runs 29 days. Therefore, she can predict approximately when her next period will begin. Once she knows when her period will likely start, she can count back 10 days to find out when her energy will be the lowest. She'll want to be sure to get plenty of sleep around that time.

As with most women with PMS, the week before Laura's period is the most difficult. With this in mind, she should be careful not to overschedule herself or her family that week. She can warn her husband when her worst days will be and ask for some extra help and support. Additionally, she can monitor her reactions and, hopefully, more readily recognize the onset of PMS rather than being confused and caught off guard by the intensity of her emotions. Once she knows she's in the grip of PMS, she can remove herself from stressful situations if possible, employ her "Don't Do" list (which we'll discuss later), and arrange for some time alone. Finally, Laura can put off making major decisions when they are most difficult for her. Waiting just a few days is often enough to restore her energy, confidence, and decisiveness.

Your chart will be as unique as you are, and it will hold powerful insights. I was amazed that an exercise that took me seconds a day provided so much information. I now know when I'm most vulnerable. I can predict when I'll feel overwhelmed and out of sorts. I know when things will be toughest in my relationship with my husband. With this knowledge, I'm actively working to develop specific strategies that will work for me and my family.

For example, last Saturday night it suddenly become very important to me that my son eat what was on his plate. Usually we have a pretty loose food policy. We simply ask our kids to take two small bites of everything. After that, they decide what they will finish… except last Saturday. I've noticed that "standing on principle" becomes much more important to me when I have PMS. Instead of the two-bite policy, it became crucial to me that my son eat all of whatever it was he didn't want to eat. Sadly, I made an issue out of it and ruined dinner for everyone. I knew I was being overly strict but couldn't seem to stop myself. Two days later, when I realized it was PMS, I felt sorry that once again I couldn't let go and that my family had borne the brunt of my moodiness. I apologized to my son. The more I notice about my behavior, however, the more I'll be able to identify what is PMS in the future. If I can't stop it, I plan to remove myself from the situation. Dinner without mom is probably better than dinner with a grumpy, irritable mom.

Though I'll likely struggle with PMS until I move through menopause, charting it is helping me manage it more proactively. Charting and making observations will help you too.

PMS S.O.S.

As Amber reviewed Callie's chart she said, "Finding solutions is the key, Callie. All the charts in the world won't do you a bit of good if you don't develop a workable strategy for responding to what you know to be true about yourself when you have PMS. It's like when Meg and I were having trouble getting along. We knew our relationship wasn't working, so we had to figure out what to do to make it work. By focusing on solving the problem, we were able to be *proactive* rather than *reactive* when it came to communicating with one another."

"What kinds of changes did you make?"

"I let Meg take more responsibility for setting her own schedule, rather than making her work around mine. I stopped running interference with teachers when she wasn't doing her work, so she had to suffer the consequences of her decisions. And I started noticing her moods more and responded accordingly. When she didn't feel like talking, I didn't force her. If she needed time away from the family, I let her have it."

"Did she make changes too?"

"She did. She agreed to let me know where she was, who she was with, and when she would be home. She agreed to focus more on her grades and even identified what privileges she would give up if she got anything lower than a 'C' on her report cards. She also committed to being proactive in telling me when she needed space, rather than expecting me to read her mind. The transformation in our relationship was amazing—and all because we took the time to agree on what we could expect from one another."

"What kind of solutions did you come up with for when you had PMS?" queried Callie.

"I've already shared that at least once a month David brings dinner home or takes us out for dinner. When the kids were young he'd call his mom and ask her to watch the kids for a morning so I could get out of the house. I often compensated for my lack of energy by taking the kids out for lunch, to a park, to the library, or another location where I could supervise them but not have to directly interact with them. I know that sounds terrible, but it was better to be honest about my limitations at that time of the month rather than pretend everything was okay. I knew it wasn't, and I chose to respond accordingly."

"I understand what you're saying, Amber. But I feel a little guilty about the idea of having to compensate like that each month. It seems like a cop out."

"Why?"

"Letting myself off the hook like that sets a bad example for my kids. And I feel like I'm not doing my job as a mother if I'm not diligent 100 percent of the time."

"Is it even realistic to expect to be 'diligent' 100 percent of the time?" Amber asked. "What's more important to you, Callie, being Supermom or being even-tempered and consistent with your children?"

"Being even-tempered and consistent, of course," Callie responded.

"Then doesn't it make sense to strive for that goal even if means making special plans on days you know you're going to struggle? If you know in advance that it's going to be tough to be the kind of mom you want to be on any given day, why not plan ahead? Why not plan to stay home that day and be gentle in setting goals and such? Or go out if it distracts the kids and makes your day run more smoothly? Or let the kids watch an extra video that day? Or stay in your pajamas until noon?" Questions rushed off Amber's tongue. "It seems to me that it's more fair to your entire family if you're proactive and responsive to what you know about yourself and your patterns when you have PMS rather than continuing to hope it won't impact them or it will get better on its own, Callie. Isn't it unrealistic to expect yourself to be emotionally, physically, and mentally prepared 100 percent every single day of the month—especially when you know there will be extenuating circumstances, such as raging hormones?"

Callie had to admit Amber was convincing. *Is handling PMS simply a matter of making different choices for me and my family?* she wondered.

Planning according to what she knew about herself didn't seem like such a big deal when she looked at it through Amber's eyes. Callie resolved to develop a plan that would address her symptoms and be good for her family. For the first time since calling Amber, Callie felt a flicker of hope that it might just be possible to live with PMS and maintain her loving disposition for her family.

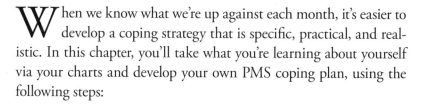

When we know what we're up against each month, it's easier to develop a coping strategy that is specific, practical, and realistic. In this chapter, you'll take what you're learning about yourself via your charts and develop your own PMS coping plan, using the following steps:

- Assess your situation.
- Anticipate your needs and activate your plan.
- Adjust your expectations when premenstrual.
- Avoid testy situations.

These steps comprise a realistic, effective, and powerful response to PMS. By recognizing what happens to you each month and planning appropriately, you can prevent many of the situations that may currently be challenging you.

Assess Your Situation

The first step in creating your plan is to *assess the situation*. Your chart will help you determine *when* you're most likely to have difficulty. At those times you focus on *what* triggers your ugliest behavior. Triggers are whatever generates explosive or extreme reactions on your part. Premenstrual women are more prone to triggers for two reasons:

- We tend to "take the negative details of a situation and blow them up, magnify them, even catastrophize them."[1]
- "[We] tend to perceive what people say and situations around [us] in an extreme way. It is all or nothing, with

little or no room for a middle ground. [We] perceive people
and events as either good or bad, wonderful or horrible."[2]

Due to our negative mind-set and extreme thinking premenstrually, what may normally not cause difficulty in our relationships often
does. Here's one mom's premenstrual mind-set:

> This time of "hormones gone mad" is giving me so much
> perspective. It made me cry last week when I got caught in
> road construction traffic. I could clearly see that hold-up
> as a deliberate plot by the Department of Transportation
> to make me late for my appointment. It made me pick a
> fight with my daughter over a really critical issue—she left
> her flipflops by the phone. I suddenly saw her sloppiness as
> a sign of my improper mothering. And my husband! He
> didn't put out the recycle bin early enough to catch the
> truck, which was clearly a sign that I'm not valuable enough
> to help and that our relationship is headed for the brink.
>
> Then *Poof!* My period finally arrived, and I woke up to a
> beautiful world. Gone was the desire to get a divorce, put
> my kids up for adoption, and quit my job.[3]

Can you identify with her extreme thinking? What are the triggers
in your life? I've identified the following triggers in mine:

- *Household clutter and messiness.* When I have PMS, things
  that normally don't bother me begin to annoy me. I'm usually willing to pick up after other family members. But
  when I'm in the clutches of PMS, shoes in the hallway,
  dishes left on the counter, and books left carelessly on the
  floor have triggered my anger. *My PMS response:* "I'm sick
  and tired of being the only one who does anything around
  this house!"

- *Arguing between my children.* My kids get along fairly well.
  When they don't, I'm used to playing referee—unless I have

PMS. When that happens, any escalation in accusations, volume, or physical horseplay usually results in a technical foul…on my part. *My PMS response:* "Why do you kids have to fight like this? It sets me off and makes me crazy! Why do you always have to bicker?"

- *Anything remotely interpreted as criticism.* When I have PMS, I hear everything through a negative filter. I interpret "When's dinner?" as a criticism of my timeliness in preparing it. "What's for dinner?" questions whether or not I'm a capable cook. "Are you going to the grocery soon?" becomes a criticism of my shopping patterns. Innocent comments and questions become gauntlets thrown down by unsuspecting family members. *My PMS response:* "I'm not your slave!"

- *Anything other than immediate and cheerful obedience.* I'm usually clear in making my expectations known to my children. I believe in being flexible and letting them decide in which order they'll do their homework, take their showers, and practice the piano…unless I have PMS. At "that time of the month," if I ask a child to do something, I expect him or her to do it immediately. If my child doesn't, a swift and instantaneous response from me occurs. *My PMS response:* "Do it—and do it *now!*"

- *Crafting, creating, and cooking.* I love doing special activities with my kids. But doing them when I have PMS is dangerous. My temper is shorter, my patience wears thin quickly, and I expect my kids to do things *my* way, which isn't usually how they want to do it. The messiness of creating together also causes trouble for me when I have PMS. *My PMS response:* "I'm trying to help you! Why do you have to be so difficult? I can't stand this."

As I write, I realize how petty my PMS responses may seem. So why do they become larger than life once a month? I know it's hormones and such, but I really don't know the specific answer to that question. Here's what I do know: Petty or not, these are real conflict-prone situations for me. When I have PMS I have to work hard to restrain myself from flying off the handle when any one of these circumstances occurs. By knowing my trouble spots, I'm more easily able to control and counter my typical PMS responses to them. In a sense I've developed a personal warning system that alerts me when I'm entering treacherous territory. As Julie Barnhill writes:

> There are warning signs and signals for just about everything that can be potentially dangerous. Train whistles and crossing lights caution motorists to slow down and be observant. Tornado sirens drone loudly as we scurry to a basement or other protective space and scan the skies for a dreaded funnel shape. However, unless you're trained to recognize these warning signs, they are ineffective in helping you remain safe and protected. You have to *know* the warning signs that spell imminent danger—especially when *you're* the one in danger of exploding in anger.[4]

Julie is right. We must train ourselves to recognize the warning signs. That's what this chapter is all about: Making an honest assessment regarding our triggers so that we can develop effective warning systems and avoid the meltdowns that we know so well as MUI.

Notice how exaggerated my responses were to the events I identified. Obviously I'm not the *only one* who does anything around our house, my kids don't *always* bicker, my family doesn't treat me like a *slave,* my kids aren't intentionally being *difficult,* and there's value in letting my children have input on their schedules without me hissing "Do it *now!*" (Unless, of course, they were asked to do something and didn't. Then I have to follow up.)

Can you imagine how confusing it is for children to be parented by "Nice Mom" most of the month and have "Mean Mom" step in for a few days of havoc and unpredictable behavior? My desire to conquer (or at least reduce) my overreaction is directly tied to my longing that my kids have a mom they can trust and count on, not one who models erratic, poor behavior.

Your triggers are unique. That's why it's important that you take the time to develop your own list, similar to what I did. Your goal is twofold: 1) identify your triggers; 2) develop a list of warning signals to alert you to proceed with caution. Some warning signals are:

- rising anger, irritability, frustration
- rage
- feeling overwhelmed
- extreme sadness
- feeling stressed

With practice I've learned that when I start feeling any of these, I need to remove myself from the situation, delay my response in some fashion, think instead of speak, or a combination of these techniques. In fact, after one verbal explosion, I looked at my kids and said, "Mommy needs a timeout!" They watched in wonder as I walked to the timeout chair and sat myself down. This was good for me and great for them to witness. Now, occasionally, one of my kids will ask me if I need a timeout. That question has also become a warning signal for me. Instead of being offended, I choose to respond positively by taking an adult timeout. (Remember, parenting experts suggest a minute of timeout for every year of age!)

Anticipate Your Needs and Activate a Plan

Once you've assessed your situation, it is necessary to *anticipate your needs* and *activate a plan* that will allow you to respond appropriately. Amber gave Callie some ideas that might be helpful to you:

- Plan dinner out unless you know dining with kids in a restaurant is one of your triggers. If it is, perhaps you can ask your spouse to pick up dinner on the way home. Or you can make and freeze meals ahead of time so preparation is easier during your volatile time of the month.

- Identify free or inexpensive activities you can do that provide a distraction for your children and allow you to supervise them from a distance.
- Declare a "no car" day. Choose not to leave the house and instead enjoy a lazy, hurry-free day.

More ideas include:

- Create a list of quiet activities at home such as "playing library," allowing special computer time, planning a movie day, or doing a puzzle parade in which your kids attempt to do every puzzle in the house.
- Arrange for a sitter on the days you know will be the worst for you. If money is a concern, consider swapping sitting responsibilities with a friend or hiring a "mother's helper," a tween that isn't yet old enough to babysit unsupervised but who can play with your children in another part of the house while you enjoy some alone time. Usually a mother's helper charges less than the going rate for babysitters. I've even been desperate enough that I paid each of my children a dollar to play quietly with one another!
- Ask your husband or another family member to help school-aged kids with homework or to drive them to evening activities so you have some down time.
- If your kids are old enough, ask them to set the table, prepare and serve dinner, and tidy the kitchen afterward.
- Go to bed earlier so you are well-rested at a time when you need all your energy reserves.

What ideas can you add based on your list of triggers? Remember, your goal is to develop a proactive plan that recognizes and addresses your personal PMS limitations.

Adjust Your Expectations

Anticipating your triggers and activating your plan also requires another important step: *adjusting your expectations.* Like Callie, you may need to give yourself permission to be less than Supermom during your period or less than "100 percent diligent" when PMS swamps you. It's also essential to adjust your expectations of other family members as well. Kids will be kids, and your husband isn't a mind reader. Be willing to cut them some slack.

Avoid Testy Situations

There's a final step in the process that will be helpful to you: *avoid testy situations.* In my case, this meant creating a "Don't Do" or a "To Don't" list. These are the things I *don't* do when I have PMS:

- *I don't shop with my kids, especially for shoes, clothes, or groceries.* Shoes test my patience because I have to get down on the ground to help slide them on and off, put my thumb on the toe to see if they fit, and watch as my kids run goofily down the aisle with the shoes hooked together by a strand of plastic. I should be able to laugh at this, like they do, but when I have PMS it just irritates me. Clothes shopping is off limits for pretty much the same reason, and grocery shopping is out of the question because of the disputes over who gets to push the cart and who gets to put the groceries into it.

- *I don't start big projects or initiate new house rules.* Both of these require more energy and attention than I usually have to give when I'm premenstrual.

- *I don't drive anywhere with my kids if I can avoid it.* Noise in the car makes me absolutely stark raving mad when I have PMS. Loud laughter, joking, horseplay, and arguing quickly get to me, usually resulting in a stern request for quiet. I've been known to pull over when the request isn't immediately honored. I try to avoid any situation that might trigger anger for me—including driving my kids around when I'm premenstrual.

- *I avoid other people's kids.* I debated whether or not to include this one because of my fear that you'll think I'm horrible for admitting it. But not only am I more impatient with my own children when I'm "under the influence," I'm also more intolerant with other people's children. Many other PMS moms shared the same thing with me, so I'm not alone.

- *I don't make big decisions.* Because I feel overwhelmed when I have PMS, I'm not in a good position to make wise decisions or to carefully think through any potential ramifications. Plus I tend to doubt myself and question my ability, making decision making even more confusing.

- *I don't examine the quality of my relationships.* Since I feel depressed when I have PMS and often have a negative outlook, it's dangerous for me to think about my relationships with family and friends. During this time of the month, they all seem to be lacking. I'm much better off addressing relationship issues when I'm feeling physically and emotionally well.

Here are three other "don't do" items shared by moms who responded to my online survey:

- *I avoid stressful relationships or social situations* during the last 4 or 5 days of my cycle because I know I can't always trust my perceptions during this time.

- *No multitasking!* Focus on one thing at a time.

- *Do not put yourself in a situation you know will be detrimental* to you mentally. For example, if you know that any time you see particular friends you compare yourself and come up short, try not to see them when you have PMS.

Since creating my "To Don't" list, I've reduced stress and saved myself (and my family and friends) a lot of unhappiness. I've also lowered my expectations of myself and others, which has prevented a great deal of the disharmony that used to be present in my home for several days each month. I trust that creating a "To Don't" list will do the same for you.

Remember the list of "Eleven Things PMS Stands For" at the end of chapter 3? When you take the time to complete the exercises in this chapter, you'll be able to add another item to the list: *Proactive Mothers Soar.* It may be a stretch, but when your self-knowledge joins with preparedness, you'll find that you need to send out fewer S.O.S. signals during PMS.

7

All Stressed Up and Everywhere to Go

As Callie rounded the corner of aisle eight in the grocery store, she heard someone cry. She glanced up in time to see a woman, presumably the mother, bent over at the waist, shaking her finger wildly at a small child.

"I told you to stop! You're making me crazy! Now get in the cart!" She lifted the child in one swift movement and deposited her forcefully into the cart. Without hesitating, she turned to the child remaining at her side.

"Don't you dare even think about asking me for one more thing. Do you understand?" The woman was loud enough that people in aisles seven and nine could likely hear. "I have enough going on in my life with your father out of town and your grandmother in the hospital. I'm missing work, I'm behind at home, and now you get sick too! Plus, we're going to be late for dinner. I can't take anymore. Don't say another word to me, okay?"

Callie doubted the child was old enough to understand the weight of his mother's words, but as a mom herself, she recognized a fellow stressed sojourner. She felt sorry for the woman and wished she could think of something to do to help, but Callie figured it was better to just roll by and not say a word. As she passed the woman, she thought about all the times her own stress had exploded in hurtful, angry words and actions she'd rather forget.

As Callie continued shopping, she thought about what the woman had said. Her husband was out of town. A grandmother was in the hospital. One of the children was sick. The woman was missing work and overwhelmed at home. With the stressors adding up, it was easy to see why she exploded. Yet Callie felt sorry for the young children who had borne the brunt of their mother's angry reaction to the pressures in her life. Then Callie felt sorry for her own children who had felt the effects of her PMS anger more times than she cared to count.

73

Have you ever been the woman in the grocery store? I have. It's stressful enough to grocery shop with young children but worse when you add additional life pressures to the picture. It makes sense that women with children have higher levels of stress-related hormones in their blood than women without children.[1] Research has also shown that stress magnifies PMS. In fact, Dr. Ron Eaker identifies stress reduction as one of the top three ways to manage PMS. Destressing is an important coping tool when it comes to managing premenstrual syndrome.

By definition, stress is the way our bodies and minds react to something that upsets our normal balance in life. And kids top the list of things that upset the "normal balance." After we have kids, is there ever such a thing as "normal" or "balance" again?

If you're a little irritable due to PMS, stress will quickly heighten that state. If you're feeling overwhelmed, stress may make you feel like you can't handle the load. And if you're angry, even a small stressor may push you into full rage. That's why it is essential to actively work to minimize or eliminate stress during your toughest days each month.

Moms have a tendency to downplay the physical and emotional stressors in their lives. I believe we've become so accustomed to continually adding to our workload that we do it without thinking. But I love what Mary LoVerde says in her book *Stop Screaming at the Microwave:* "When you add and add and add in mathematics, it's called infinity. When you add and add and add in life, it's called insanity!" Many of us are living insane lives. But often *we don't recognize it.* We think burning the candle at both ends, not getting enough sleep, and relying on caffeine to get us through our days are normal.

It's not. Nor should it be.

I spoke with a woman who burst into tears when I asked what kind of pressure she was under at home. She described the stress of raising three special-needs children, one of whom is autistic. She also had the responsibility of leading a women's group at her church and was an officer in her local parent/teacher organization. In her "spare" time, she helped do the books for her husband's business while providing occasional transportation for her father-in-law, who no longer drove. The stressors in *her* life were enough to make *me* want to take a nap! But when I probed further, I realized she thought her activity level was normal and felt she couldn't do anything about it. She didn't recognize that her high activity level, combined with her lack of taking control over it, was a potentially lethal combination. She was miserable but didn't feel she could—or deserved—to do anything about it.

Because many of us are "can do" women, we don't often take the time to objectively evaluate our stress level. And when we do take the time to notice it, we sometimes feel helpless about doing anything about it. Therefore we don't do anything at all—except put our nose to the grindstone, pledging to work even harder and longer. Take a look at the following list of "mom" issues that influence our stress level:

- number of children (the more children, the higher the stress)
- any special needs (physical or learning disabilities or illness)
- overall level of support from children and spouse
- workload (inside or outside the home or both)
- ages of children (the younger the children, the more physical the stress; the older the children, the more the emotional stress)
- financial well-being (or lack thereof)
- additional care-giving responsibilities (aging parents, other family members)
- presence of marital discord
- ability to multitask effectively

- self-imposed and/or unrealistic deadlines
- strong desire to be a great mom

The more of these stressors you experience, the more cognizant you need to be premenstrually.

If you feel you can't get a grip on stress in your life for yourself, would you be willing to do it for your kids? My children motivate me to regularly review our schedule and trim what's unnecessary and stressful. In addition, through trial and error, I've learned how important it is to limit my personal commitments at times.

Children learn what they live. What are they seeing in your life? A daily mad dash from one activity to another without any downtime in between? Or do they see a well-paced schedule that allows for meals together, family fun nights, and occasional lazy strolls around the block that provide opportunities for your children to talk about what's going on in their world?

You are the author of your life. What kind of story are you writing? What kind of stressors are you living with? Pause a moment and ponder those questions. Making a list might help clarify this for you.

Since we know that stress is a PMS stronghold, we are wise to pay attention to its effects on our lives. What's stressing you right now? And, more importantly, what are you going to do about it?

Deeply ingrained habits and thought patterns directly affect your stress level. When you believe you can't change something, you won't even try. But even when you can't change your circumstance, you can change your response to it. And when you change your habits, you change your stress level. Here are some small actions that will pay big dividends for you as a "PMS Momma."

Eliminate "I can't" from your vocabulary. The words "I can't" are extremely disempowering. The more you use them, the more you believe them. Often the word "can't" itself is a stressor because it results in negative thinking. Focus instead on what you *can* do. If you *can't* get out of hosting your extended family each year for the holidays, you *can* decide that this year it will be a potluck with paper plates or that you'll ask a niece to set the table and your nephews to do the dishes after each meal. In this case you're turning "I can't get out of hosting the holiday meal" to "I can't get out of hosting the holidays, but *I can* ask for help in preparing and cleaning up after all the meals."

Be aware of the "shoulds" in your life. As I wrote in *How to Say No... and Live to Tell About It:*

> Doing things because you think you should is a lousy reason. First, it doesn't take into consideration your gifts or abilities. Second, it doesn't reflect your calendar and how busy you currently are. Third, "shoulds" encourage us to do things because others are doing them or so that we don't feel guilty rather than because we want to or are gifted in a particular area. Fourth, "should" suggests that we have no choice, when in fact we always do. And finally, and most importantly, the Bible warns against giving to others reluctantly or under compulsion. Second Corinthians 9:7 says, "Each man should give what he has decided in his heart to give, not reluctantly or under compulsion, for God loves a cheerful giver."[2]

Many times I've done things because I think I "should." Because I'm not doing them for the right reasons (i.e., I want to, I'm good at it, I'm excited about it), my efforts are less than they "should" be or I don't do the task cheerily and that, in and of itself, causes stress. Consequently, I've learned that doing something because I feel I "should" invites unnecessary stress into my life. When I hear myself think or say the word "should," my personal warning system goes off, and I'm extra careful about the decision I make.

Be intentional about what you say yes to. When you say yes to something in life, you automatically say no to something else. That's why it's important to know the price of your yes. Agreeing to let a child play on a competitive, traveling sports team may mean saying no to leisurely weekends or to a family vacation during the sports season. When you understand the price of your yes, it's easier to make commitments that don't later cause stress. Intentional yeses also allow you to live in harmony with your values, which also reduces stress.

Commit to getting as much sleep as you need on a regular basis. This is one area where women especially try to gain more hours in their days—by giving up sleep. According to the National Sleep Foundation's 2007 "Sleep in America Poll," when pressed for time, 52 percent of the 1,003 women polled responded that sleep is one of the first things they sacrifice when the day runs out before their "To Do" list does.[3] Fatigue causes stress, so being well-rested is one way to keep tension at bay.

Several women who responded to my online survey indicated that "going to bed early" is one way they respond to PMS. Even if you can't get to bed early regularly, perhaps you can commit to doing it when you're premenstrual.

Overcome "just one more thingitis." This disease deludes you into believing that if you can get "just one more thing done" you'll be a) happier, b) more effective, c) richer, d) sexier, or e) all of these. I have a chronic case of this, which often keeps me from getting out of the house in a timely fashion, which results in a hurried dash to wherever I need to be. I'm ashamed to admit that this happened so often when my kids were young that the words, "Hurry up, we're going to be late" became my mantra. Now, sadly, when we leave the house one of my kids will often ask, "Are we going to be late?" I regret this.

"Just one more thingitis" also keeps me up late at night due to the false belief that if I get "just one more thing" done before going to bed tonight, tomorrow will be easier. This is a falsehood, and delaying my bedtime interferes with my sleep needs.

Ask for help. I personally stink at this, so this is a case of "do as I say, not as I do." I'm working on it though! Why is it so hard to ask for help? Here's a list from my book *The Mother Load: How to Meet Your Own Needs While Caring for Your Family:*

- Asking for help means admitting we can't handle everything on our own.
- Soliciting help makes us indebted to another person.
- Requesting help means giving up control.
- We think mothering is our job and no one else's; therefore, we feel compelled to do it by ourselves.
- We don't want to burden others.
- We believe we're the only ones who can do it "right."
- We've been disappointed in the past when we have asked for help and others have let us down.
- Sometimes it's easier to do it on our own.[4]

Slowly but surely I'm seeing that asking for help doesn't make me less than I am, but instead makes me *more than I am on my own.* The more I focus on how effective I can be when I ask for help, the less I focus on the fact that I need help in the first place. It's getting easier for me to say, "I need help. Could you? Would you?" Plus it gives the other person an opportunity to be blessed by helping.

Lighten your load when you have PMS. If there's ever been a legitimate excuse to slow down and take it easy, this is it. Since we know PMS magnifies stress, and stress can lead to poor interactions with our children, it's really for their sakes that we need to give ourselves a break. In this case, what's good for us is ultimately good for our family.

Managing my family's schedule usually comes easy for me. It's less so when I have PMS. Activities that require dropping off, picking up, arranging, confirming, remembering, and attending complicate life and make it more difficult to get to the end of the day in one piece.

Some survey respondents have already caught on to the value of lightening their loads to reduce stress. As you read previously, they shared PMS coping mechanisms such as "I try to schedule less and keep it simple," "I try not to push myself to do all my chores," and "I schedule more 'me' time." These are wise women.

Heed your "To Don't" list. In the last chapter you made a list of things you shouldn't do when you have PMS. Pay careful attention to this list and don't do the activities you identified. This reduces stress on your "black days."

Act on what you know about your kids. This is probably one of the best ways to eliminate self-induced stress. I've spoken with many women who intuitively know what their children need but don't necessarily see that they get it. When kids don't get what they need, stress ensues. (Note that I said "when kids don't get what they *need*" not "when kids don't get what they *want*." This is an important distinction.) Here's an example of what moms have told me they know about their kids—and what they do as a result (in parentheses):

- My kids need a little breathing space when they get home from school. (I don't plan any activities until after four o'clock on school days.)

- My son needs to eat every three to four hours. (I carry raisins or Cheerios in my purse at all times.)

- My daughter needs at least nine hours of sleep a night. (We routinely turn down opportunities that will get her to bed too late or require her to get up too early.)

- My daughter prefers one-on-one activities rather than large-group activities. (We let her drop out of dance and signed her up for private music lessons. We let her have one friend at a time spend the night instead of encouraging a multi-person slumber party.)

- My son thinks he's stupid. (We don't correct him by saying, "That's not right." Instead we say, "Let's take a look at problem number two again." This small change in wording has increased his confidence.)

Some of these may seem trivial. But let's say you're the mom of the child who has to be completely naked before he poops. (This is more common than you might think.) You have PMS. He needs to strip down to go to the bathroom; you're irritable and in a hurry to get your errands started. What's going to happen? The resulting stress may cause you to blow up. If you've identified this scenario as a potential trigger, however, instead of tapping your foot and hurrying your child along, you'll remove yourself from the situation and fold laundry, make a phone call, or grab a book and read a chapter while he goes about his business in the buff.

Since we know children often act up when they are tired, hungry, or have a need that's not being met, we can anticipate and prevent fatigue or hunger—the biggest reasons for poor behavior. And when you identify a need that's not being met and quickly meet it, you'll reduce everyone's stress.

Sometimes a child's need is as simple as a pat on the back, a hug, or comforting words. Sometimes it's more complicated. I've learned that I'm sometimes unwilling or incapable of meeting my children's simplest needs when I have PMS. And it's even tougher to meet their needs when none of us knows what they are. Then it's up to the parents to figure it out.

When I have PMS, I often have to force myself to 1) care about my kids' needs and 2) do something about them. I'm not proud of this, but it's the truth. PMS makes it difficult for me to do what normally comes naturally. Other PMS moms have told me they also struggle with this type of monthly apathy. Ignoring what I know about my children—and refusing to act on it—has led to more meltdowns (on my part and theirs) than I care to remember. Acting on what we know about ourselves and our children is a valuable way to reduce stress at "that time of the month."

In addition to these stress reduction tips, there are four other influences worth considering.

Level of control: The more control you feel you have in life, the less stress you'll likely have. Practice identifying and exercising the control you do have—not so that you can control others but to create a sane and meaningful life for you and your loved ones. By exercising the control you do have, you'll strengthen your response in preparation for the times you have to fight to gain even a small amount of control over a situation.

Expectations: Unrealistic expectations and those that haven't been verbalized often go unmet, resulting in stress. Carefully examine your expectations, weed out or adjust those that are unrealistic, and be sure to share your hopes with those closest to you in order to avoid misunderstandings and dashed dreams.

Fear: Often we act from a place of fear without even knowing it. We're afraid life will pass us by, that opportunities are "once in a lifetime," or that if we don't say yes, we'll lose friends. This encourages us to commit to things simply because we're afraid of what we'll miss if we don't. Operating out of fear means responding to life from a position of weakness. It's better to choose to be in charge, even if it means deliberately passing up opportunities or delaying decisions based on current life situations and circumstances. As for the friends we may lose if we don't say yes, true friends accept the word no.

Circumstances: Though we can control our responses to the circumstances we find ourselves in, we can't always control the circumstances themselves. The following have been identified as the "Top Ten Stressors."[5] If you're experiencing any of them, or a combination of them, acknowledge that your stress level is higher than usual and requires extra patience and proactive planning to reduce the ongoing effects.

- death of spouse
- divorce
- marital separation
- jail term

- death of a close family member
- personal injury or illness
- marriage
- job loss
- marital reconciliation
- retirement

Whether we're experiencing any of these or simply wrestling with a list of overwhelming demands on our lives, it's essential that we master the art of stress management. Not only will it reduce the possibility that we'll behave in a way we'll later regret, doing so allows us to model excellent life skills for our children.

Stress is real and affects us physically and emotionally. If you find yourself all stressed up with everywhere to go, that's a sure sign you need to pause and rethink things. Regularly do a stress check with the goals of reducing and eliminating whatever you can and developing coping mechanisms to handle whatever's left in a way that's positive and healthy.

If I Am What I Eat, Does That Make Me a Donut?

Callie padded to the refrigerator and reached for her morning Mountain Dew. It was a habit she'd started in college. She'd tried many times to substitute a glass of water, but she loved the "pssh" of the soda can opening first thing in the morning and the cooling refreshment she felt as the first sip flowed down her dry throat. Plus, she was addicted to the caffeine. She knew she couldn't afford the calories and had gone through a period of testing a variety of diet drinks in hopes of finding one that satisfied her like "The Dew," but none did. So she started each morning with caffeine and sugar, a habit she despised but had not yet had the courage or fortitude to break.

Callie's chiropractor had lectured her several times about starting her day with sugar, but she let his words roll off her back. She convinced herself that the damage was minimal and that she deserved to start her day with a soda due to the stresses of motherhood. It wasn't until she heard Jessica ask for a Mountain Dew for breakfast one morning that she had second thoughts. Yet she still reached for the green can every morning, pledging that she'd get rid of the habit "someday."

Today was Saturday, and Callie was the only one awake. As she surveyed the kitchen counter, she noticed the box of Krispy Kreme donuts she'd bought from a neighborhood Key Club member to help support the local food bank. As she put a donut on a plate, she thought about the irony of ingesting a donut purchased so that someone else could eat. After the first donut disappeared quickly, she had a second, minimizing the action by thinking, *The sooner we eat these, the sooner the temptation will be gone.* She'd been using this rationalization for years.

She'd been a healthy weight when she graduated from college but had been steadily gaining ever since. Callie lost her baby weight after having Abby but hadn't after Jessica. She was simply too tired and too overwhelmed to make the time for physical activity. She'd often snack intermittently throughout the morning and grab the leftovers off her kids' plates as she put the dishes in the dishwasher.

Callie loved salty, crunchy foods, preferring them to healthier alternatives such as fruits and nuts. Lately she'd started buying more fruit at the grocery store, hoping that the availability would make it easier for her to grab a healthy snack. So far it was working, but she didn't know how long the new trend would last. She'd tried to snack more wisely many times in the past, but she always ended up grabbing for the potato chips. As she thought about it, she realized there might be a connection to her period. She sensed she was able to eat well most of the month, but when PMS hit, she was back to heavily buttered popcorn, chips, and candy. As she pondered the possible connection, she decided to chart her food intake along with her mood and symptoms. If she could determine a pattern to her eating, maybe she could be more deliberate in her choices. And if she could adapt her eating habits, maybe she could drop a few pounds. Though she hadn't been motivated to do anything about it, the extra weight bothered her, making her feel unattractive and less fit. Plus, keeping up was harder than it used to be.

After Callie wrote "2 donuts" on her PMS chart, she picked up the box of remaining Krispy Kremes and dropped them in the trash. Just because she paid for them didn't mean she had to eat them. She decided the best way to deal with the temptation was to get rid of it. The small gesture made her feel good. As she walked out of the kitchen, she grabbed a banana and pledged to have it for her mid-morning snack.

Callie is on the right track by recording her food intake. After a month of tracking, she will likely see food patterns that aren't helping her PMS, and may, in fact, be making it worse. It's possible that her emotions and hormonal changes lead to food choices that increase her PMS symptoms each month.

I was surprised that nutrition repeatedly showed up in my research as an important element in managing PMS. I had no idea how much food affects symptoms. Here's some of what I learned:

- The *Journal of Reproductive Medicine* notes that women who report symptoms of PMS consume three times the amount of sugar as women who do not report symptoms.[1]
- Being overweight may possibly increase the symptoms of PMS.[2]
- Fluctuations in blood sugar may aggravate PMS symptoms.
- Many of the foods we eat can worsen PMS.

Not only can our diet determine our physical and emotional health, it may determine our PMS health as well.

Writing about this topic has challenged me to watch what I put in my mouth. I've been appalled by three things I've learned:

- I do a lot of "mindless eating," meaning I eat out of habit without paying attention to the nutritional value of what I put into my mouth.
- I don't routinely determine what constitutes a "serving," which sometimes causes me to consume larger portions than I need.
- I often use PMS as an excuse for poor eating, falsely believing that a candy bar or potato chips will make me feel better.

It's easy to convince myself that I "deserve" whatever and however much I want to eat because PMS makes me feel so bad otherwise. Noticing these things about my eating habits has made me more mindful and careful. I have a ways to go to completely change my habits, but I'm working on it. What about you? What have you noticed now? Then see what you notice after you keep a food chart in conjunction with your PMS symptoms. You may be surprised!

PMS Wise

The good news is that foods that constitute a healthy diet also comprise a good PMS diet. Focus on lean protein, fiber, complex carbohydrates (grains, colorful fruits and vegetables), and "good" fats such as those from nuts and fish. When you do this, you'll be healthier PMS wise.

In addition to the importance of choosing healthy food, I also learned there are foods that may aggravate PMS symptoms. They include:

- alcohol
- beef
- black tea
- bouillon
- butter
- catsup
- chocolate
- coffee
- commercial salad dressing
- eggs
- hot dogs
- lamb
- pork
- soft drinks
- salt
- sugar
- white bread
- white noodles
- white rice
- white-flour pastries
- whole cow's milk
- yogurt (regular)

Here's why these foods heighten PMS:

- *Caffeinated beverages* increase anxiety, irritability and mood swings and deplete the body's stores of vitamin B—interfering with carbohydrate metabolism.

- *Dairy products* interfere with the absorption of magnesium, a mineral that can decrease cramps, help glucose metabolism, stabilize mood swings, and decrease the liver's efficiency in metabolizing hormones. [Both dieticians who reviewed this information for me stressed that many women don't get the recommended amount of calcium, which may help reduce fluid retention and regulate mood-related brain chemicals. Instead of eliminating dairy products from your diet, consider selecting low or no-fat versions.]

- *Chocolate* worsens mood swings and intensifies sugar craving. [And to think that many of us use chocolate as comfort food to help our mood!] However, dark chocolate has flavonoids which are antioxidants and, when consumed in moderation, can help maintain heart health.

- *Sugar* depletes the body's B-complex vitamins and minerals and intensifies sugar craving.

- *Alcohol* depletes the body's vitamin B and minerals, disrupts carbohydrate metabolism, and can disrupt the liver's ability to metabolize hormones, causing higher-than-normal estrogen.

- *Beef, pork and lamb* may have a high fat content. Look for lean cuts of these types of meat, such as the loin or round.

- *Salt and high-sodium foods* (such as bouillon, salad dressings, catsup, and hot dogs) all worsen fluid retention, bloating and breast tenderness.[3]

Did you notice that many of these foods are "comfort foods," those we turn to when we're feeling bad or need a pick-me-up? Though they do produce a temporary mood upswing, many also result in a later put-you-down (especially simple sugars such as those found in cookies, candy, ice cream) when your blood sugar quickly rises and then drops after eating them. Instead of grabbing cookies next time you have a PMS craving, grab some fruit. This will help you avoid the swift drop in blood sugar that makes you vulnerable to PMS symptoms such as exhaustion, restlessness, irritability, and foggy thinking.

Sugar-laden foods result in wildly fluctuating blood sugar. Eat lean proteins, fiber, and complex carbohydrates. Their complex structure is more slowly broken down in the digestive process, causing blood sugar levels to rise slowly, peak more slowly, and fall slowly—stabilizing mood, cravings, and energy. Healthy food choices include:

- fresh fruits
- fresh vegetables
- whole grains
- lean meats
- poultry
- fish
- soy products
- brown rice
- whole grain pasta
- potatoes
- yams
- seeds
- nuts
- vegetable or seed oil
- low- or nonfat dairy products
- water
- decaffeinated tea and coffee[4]

In addition to carefully choosing the *type* of food you eat, notice the *frequency* with which you eat. According to Lori Futterman, RN, "Eating about every three to four hours in small amounts can regulate your blood sugar more readily than eating the traditional 'three squares' each day. This blood sugar control helps regulate your mood and some of the physical premenstrual symptoms, such as cravings."[5]

Diet and fitness expert Harley Pasternak agrees: "Eating five meals a day—and eating the right combination of foods—can prevent your body from releasing excess insulin into its system. By eating five normal-size meals instead of the usual two or three big meals, you tend to eat less food at each meal...As a result, less insulin is released and you store less fat."[6]

When my children were preschool age, I always made sure they had a snack between breakfast and lunch and one between lunch and dinner. Though I didn't understand then why it was important for them to eat frequently, now I do. By feeding them more often, I helped them avoid a rapid drop in their blood sugar level, preventing the meltdowns that occurred if too much time elapsed between snacks and meals. Even though we're adults, we obviously have the same need to maintain a healthy blood sugar level. Eating the right foods every three to four hours will help minimize PMS symptoms.

Since learning about the importance of having an even blood sugar level, I've given myself permission to eat between meals and have deliberately started stocking healthy snacks. Instead of waiting until I'm hungry, I watch the clock and try to eat every three to four hours, as recommended. I've noticed if I wait until I'm hungry, I'm likely to eat more than I need or grab whatever's most convenient rather than what's best. In addition, instead of looking in the pantry first, I'm making myself go to the fruit bin in the refrigerator or grab some nuts.

As you adopt more "PMS friendly" eating habits, consider writing down what you consume. Harley Pasternak notes, "Seeing a few weeks' worth of food logs that show how much better you're eating can be the inspiration you need to stay the course. In fact it's been shown that people who keep track of what they eat are more successful with their nutritional goals."[7]

Writing down what you eat may help you discover that the diet you think is rich in lean protein, fiber, and complex carbohydrates really isn't. Or that unhealthy snacking is sabotaging your healthy meals. Or that cravings for less-healthy foods occur regularly in conjunction with your menstrual cycle, requiring deliberate effort and careful planning to keep you from succumbing to monthly binges or sugar overloads.

Though many women benefit by writing down everything they eat, there is a caveat. I've found that the more I focus on what I'm eating, the more obsessed I become with food. Writing things down makes me fixate on food so I end up eating more than usual. Plus, concerned that my diary will point to favorite foods I'll have to give up, I tend to consume more of them, falsely believing I'll never get to eat them again. (The mind is a powerful foe or ally!)

Because we're all different, our approach to food will be different. If keeping a food diary helps you, do it. But if doing so is likely to backfire on you, then don't.

As you implement nutritional changes, consider what Danna Demetre, author of *The Heat Is On: Health, Humor & Hope for Women Facing Menopause,* writes:

> Most women take an all-or-nothing approach to nutrition and dieting. That is, they are either on a "health binge" or off. If you get one thing out of this chapter, I hope it is that small improvements made daily will truly add up. It's more beneficial to improve your nutrition by 10 or 20 percent for the rest of your life than it is to eat perfectly for a month or two and then fall back into your old habits.[8]

You probably don't need to overhaul your diet in one week. If changes in your diet will help control PMS symptoms, introduce small, easy changes first. When these small changes have become part of your regular routine, move on to more challenging ones. Success in making small changes leads to a greater chance for success in making bigger changes.

From Mindless to Mindful

As you consider the impact of your personal diet, there are two other issues to pay attention to. First is your water intake. Are you getting enough? Experts recommend at least four ounces every hour you are awake.[9] If you wait to drink until you're thirsty, your body's fluids are already depleted. Consequently, you should be watching the clock to signal when you should be eating and when you should be drinking water. Almost every cell in your body needs water to function properly. When you don't drink enough, your body resorts to handling the most essential functions first. In addition, water helps you feel full longer, so adequate hydration helps with weight control.

Another aspect of weight control is portion control. Since we know that excess body weight contributes to an increase in PMS symptoms, it's essential that as we watch *what* we eat and *how often* we eat, we also note *how much* we consume. As little as a few extra pounds can affect how we feel on a daily basis—and the severity of our premenstrual problems. By monitoring what we put in our mouths, we can indirectly exercise some control over what happens to us during the luteal, or the week before menstruating, phase of our cycle. Here's what one mom learned about her portion sizes:

> Several years ago I did some "experimenting" with fasting. One of the things I learned through that experience was that I was eating way more food than I needed in a day to live. I think we all use food to help us deal with emotions and stress, and really it's a dangerous addiction to get involved with. I think God gave us food to live, and I believe he gave us food to enjoy (thus taste buds), but many times in this consumerized and stressed out world we live in we use it for so much more.
>
> I eat several small meals or snacks during the day. I think about what I'll feel like after I eat something—will it make me feel better, will it nourish my body, make me stronger, etc., or will I feel worse afterward? I bear in mind that in my job I burn very few calories sitting and listening to people every day, so I try to not consume more calories than I burn.

Though I'm not necessarily suggesting fasting, I think it's interesting to note what this mom discovered: She was eating more than necessary, and sometimes eating for the wrong reasons. This knowledge enabled her to transform her personal relationship with food from mindless to mindful.

As you consider your own eating habits, it's helpful to note that typical portion sizes have increased over the years, spurred on by the "super-size" mentality. In fact, "fountain sodas during the 1950s and 1960s were about seven ounces, compared with 12 to 64 ounces these days. A typical bag of popcorn at the movies was once about five to six cups. Now a large bucket with butter flavor contains up to 20 cups and 1,640 calories. A pasta entrée at a restaurant? Double what it used to be. Eating at home? Standard plates, bowls and glasses are bigger, too."[10] Knowing that plates and portion sizes are larger today makes it easier to leave food on your plate—or to put less on to begin with.

According to the Utah Department of Health, one way to approach the issue of portion control is by "dividing your plate," which is an easy way to meet healthful dietary recommendations. Fill half your plate with fruits and vegetables, one-fourth with meat, fish, or another protein source, and the remaining fourth with grains or starchy vegetables. Some companies today are selling "portion plates" that have divided sections and guidelines for size control printed right on them. If a "divided plate" is too general for your taste, there are two other methods of portion control that might be helpful as you picture how much you should be eating:

> *Hands-on portion control* helps you measure your helpings based on the size of your hand. Here are examples of appropriate portions:
>
> - 3 ounces of meat, fish, or poultry (the size of the palm of your hand)
> - ¼ cup mixed nuts or granola (equal to 1 layer on your palm)
> - 1 cup veggies or berries (the size of a tight fist)
> - 1 cup popcorn or cereal flakes (the equivalent of 2 cupped hands)
> - ½ cup rice or pasta (a rounded handful)
> - ½ teaspoon oil or butter (equal to 1 fingertip)[11]
>
> *Comparative portion control* measures food against the size of common household items:
>
> - 3 ounces of meat, poultry, or fish = deck of cards
> - 2 tablespoons of peanut butter = one unshelled walnut

- 2 tablespoons of salad dressing = shot glass
- 1 teaspoon of olive oil = standard cap size on a 16-ounce water bottle
- 1 teaspoon of butter = standard postage stamp
- 1 cup cold cereal = baseball
- ½ cup rice or pasta = ½ baseball
- 1 ounce hard cheese = 4 dice
- 1 potato = computer mouse
- 1 piece of fruit = baseball[12]

Another portion resource that's both fun and easy to use is at www. mypyramid.gov. Enter your age, weight, and height and receive a personalized printout to guide your servings, portion sizes, and food choices, as well as an in-depth listing of the types of healthy foods that comprise each category.

These lists certainly make it easier to determine how much we should be eating. If you're like me, you realize that somewhere along the way your portions became distorted. As a result of my research for this chapter, I'm now dishing up my plate, and then removing some of what I originally placed on it. If I'm still hungry after clearing my plate, I allow myself to have more. Most often, though, I'm satisfied after the first round.

In addition to helping with your own weight control, paying attention to portions has a benefit for your family too. Nearly 35 percent of American children ages 6 to 19 are overweight. Half of those—some 11 million—are so overweight they're classified as obese. Over the last 25 years, the obesity rate has *doubled* for young children and *tripled* for teenagers. Childhood obesity often leads to adult obesity, and overweight children have a 70 percent chance of becoming overweight adults.[13] There's a good chance that the habits you're establishing with your children now will follow them into adulthood. I've become more mindful of my own eating as I watch how my children eat. I'm well aware that I influence their habits—and I don't always like what I see.

The Big Three

Nutrition is one of the "big three" when it comes to managing PMS symptoms, along with *stress reduction* and *physical activity.* Don't underestimate the effect food…or just eating…has on your mood and emotions. There's a direct connection between what you eat and drink and how you feel. As you evaluate the role nutrition plays in influencing your PMS each month, remember that you can reduce symptoms by:

- focusing on eating lean protein, fiber, and complex carbo-hydrates
- limiting caffeinated beverages, dairy products (unless they are low- or no-fat), sugar, alcohol, high-fat meats, salt, and high-sodium foods
- eating every three to four hours to maintain a constant blood sugar level
- keeping a food log
- making small improvements in your eating habits rather than radical changes
- drinking four ounces of water every hour you are awake
- practicing portion control
- leading by example. Your kids are watching!

You've Got to Move It, Move It!

Callie walked briskly behind the stroller. It was built for one, but both girls were tucked inside, Abby in back and Jessica in front. Each had a juice box and a bag of Cheerios.

It had been a rough morning. Jessica woke at 5:00 AM and, though Callie brought her to her own bed and snuggled with her, neither were able to go back to sleep. At breakfast Jessica spilled her milk while reaching for a napkin. Callie saw the glass tip and reached across the table to prevent the spill. In the process, she spilled her own orange juice. Though she wasn't angry with Jessica, she was angry with herself for her own carelessness. As milk and juice puddled on the floor, Callie felt her physical and emotional reserves drain. Rather than waiting for the other shoe to drop, she decided to be proactive, resulting in this early morning walk.

As she moved along, Callie noticed the leaves were beginning to turn. Though fall was Callie's favorite time of year, she hadn't really noticed it since the girls came along. She used to love to scamper through the wildlife sanctuary near her home as a child and collect handfuls of colorful leaves to bring home and show her mom and dad. She was amazed by the nuances of color that burst forth at the hint of winter on its way. She remembered sitting on the front porch sorting the leaves by color and marveling at how something that was once green could turn such a bright yellow or deep red or brilliant mahogany.

As Callie pictured herself on the porch, she remembered one of her favorite childhood books: *The Fall of Freddie the Leaf*, by Leo Buscaglia. Her grandmother read it to her shortly after Callie's grandfather passed away. Callie was eight and consumed with grief. She didn't know how her grandmother could stand the loss. When Callie asked about it, her grandmother pulled the book from a shelf, cuddled next to Callie on the sofa, and read her the words that would soon be etched in her memory: "Freddie was surrounded by hundreds of other leaves just like himself, or so it seemed. Soon he discovered that no two leaves were alike, even though they were on the same tree. Alfred was the leaf next to him. Ben was the leaf on his right side, and Clare was the lovely leaf overhead."

As Callie pushed the stroller, she stared up at the trees, looking for a leaf that could be Alfred, one that could be Ben, and one that could be Clare. She smiled at her silliness. Being a mother had added so much joy to her life, but it also made her more serious, more intent, more deliberate, and a lot less spontaneous. For just a moment she longed to be a kid on her front porch again, sorting leaves. She made a mental note to take the girls to the walking trails in the local park when the leaves were at their peak this year. She'd also show them how she sorted them as a child. She thought it might be fun to relearn how to press leaves, a talent she'd long since forgotten. Maybe she'd even get a copy of *Freddie the Leaf* to share with the girls.

Callie's morning frustration dissipated with each step. The girls rested quietly in the stroller, giving Callie much-needed quiet. Walking felt good, and she chided herself for not doing it more often. She wondered when exercise had fallen off her agenda and realized that it had happened with the arrival of the girls.

She recalled how she and Steve had met while running in the wildlife sanctuary. They passed each other often during early morning workouts. She'd noticed him right away and offered a friendly smile each time he passed. This continued for months. She liked the easy grin he offered in return and responded warmly to his quips: "Great day for a run, huh?" and "Wouldn't if be great if we could bottle this weather?"

The more Callie saw Steve, the more interested she became in getting to know him. Yet she had no idea how to suggest it. Then one fateful morning she saw Steve's glove drop from his pocket, giving her an excuse to stop him. He thanked her and, as he turned to resume his run, Callie blurted, "Any interest in walking these woods together some day?" As he responded with his easy smile, Callie stammered, "I…um…I just feel like I'd like to get to know your name and more about you since I see you here so much." They met the next morning for their first walk, and the morning after for their first run together. Though he was quicker, he paced himself so they stayed together on the trail. They'd been together ever since.

Callie sighed as she thought about how the years had worn down their affection for one another. She still loved Steve, but she realized she wasn't nearly as eager to show it as she had once been. She wondered if it was possible to rejuvenate something that had become so routine. She feared that years of living with her had changed Steve's feelings, yet she was afraid to talk about it. She didn't want to rock the boat. It felt safer to just keep on as they were. She wondered, *If Steve and I found a way to exercise together again, would we reconnect?* Maybe she'd start by inviting him to take a walk around the block with her and the girls after dinner tonight. The thought energized her, and she resolved to act on the idea rather than just think about it.

As Callie rounded the corner, she wondered how it was possible to feel sentimental, sad, and hopeful all at the same time. Regardless, she felt better than she had when she'd left home that morning. She decided to walk with the girls more often.

E very physician I interviewed and every book I read indicated there are three very effective ways to manage PMS. Can you guess what they are? Yup. Stress reduction, nutrition, and exercise. *The things we're stressed about or too busy to find time to do are the very things we need.* Oh, the irony!

The three main reasons we don't exercise are:

- We can't find the time.
- We are too tired.
- We think it's boring.

I know that you know you should be exercising. And I also know that just because someone says you should doesn't mean you actually will. So instead of focusing on convincing you that you should (other than highlighting the benefits of reducing PMS-related symptoms), I'll focus on how exercise reduces PMS and offer suggestions for finding the time to do it.

If you're currently exercising on a regular basis, good for you! If you're not, I hope the following will challenge you to change your habits so you'll be around and healthy enough to hold your grandchildren someday.

Let's take a look at how exercise reduces PMS. Pamela Smith, a registered dietician, writes:

> Exercise has the amazing ability to restore your energy level, regardless of whether you are suffering from fatigue, anxiety, or depression. It will calm and soothe you. And the good news is that you feel energy and mood-altering benefits the instant you start to exercise...
>
> Because of the interconnected nature of the muscular system, brain, and other processes of the body, being sedentary depresses your mood, your thinking, and your ability to work productively. But moderate regular exercise can create a change in that biochemistry, launching you into a state of confidence and exhilaration and boosting your energy, moods and alertness. There's strong evidence that moderate exercise—a brisk walk, a forty-five minute strength workout—also triggers the release of the "pleasure chemicals" known as endorphins. In addition, working up a good sweat activates the "feel good" neurotransmitters dopamine and serotonin, which...reduce the intensity of just about every perimenopausal symptom. It can tame even the worst case of PMS![1]

Since taming PMS is our goal, it appears that exercise is a must. Here's what authors Futterman and Jones wrote:

> Being physically fit is associated with elevated mood and enhanced positive feeling. If you are fit, you are also likely to have a higher level of self-regard, and that can help you cope with PMS symptoms effectively. The research on the relationship between exercise and PMS indicates that it decreases a number of premenstrual symptoms. Aerobic

exercise that lasts thirty to forty minutes four to five times weekly has been found to effectively reduce PMS symptoms and can be as effective as a mild antidepressant medication in elevating mood.[2]

The challenge is to find exercise that interests you and a way to make the time to do it. Though you may be "too tired" to exercise regularly, once you begin you'll see that doing so leads to increased energy. *The very thing we're too tired to do is what will give us more energy.* (God certainly has a sense of humor, doesn't He!)

Before we go any further, what's your response to the idea of exercise? Do you know you need to do it but you're not interested? Do you want to but can't figure out how to fit it in? Does the concept turn you off? Does it make you feel guilty or result in negative thinking about your body? Does it stress you out because it's "one more thing" for your To-Do list?

Many women have shared with me that they make exercise more difficult than it has to be simply by what they *think* about it. If they'd stop thinking about it and go for a walk instead, the issue would go away. Seriously, many of us spend much energy thinking about exercise, feeling guilty about not doing it, wishing we could find the time, and berating ourselves because we didn't get to the gym. What if we simply put on our exercise shoes or pick up a pair of hand weights? Once we've taken the first step, momentum may carry us to the next one (heading out the door for a walk or moving our biceps to strengthen our muscles).

Effortless Doing

Instead of making exercise a chore, what if we focused on ways to naturally include it in our lives rather than having to set aside large chunks of time to do it? By "effortlessly" including physical activity in our schedules, we can take away some of the stigma or reluctance we sometimes feel when we think about it. For instance, realize that we don't have to work out a full hour for it to count. We don't have to run five miles instead of walking three to make a difference in our lives. Let's focus on how we can squeeze 10-minute workouts into our daily schedule, wearing a pedometer and walking an additional 1000 steps each day, or taking the stairs instead of the elevator whenever possible, and parking further away from the stores.

Instead of making exercise an ordeal, how can you "effortlessly" add it to your life? There's value in thinking about—and answering— this question. What's the *least* you can do to exercise more regularly? Get it on your schedule? Ask your kids to join you for a "talk around the block" after dinner? Put the stroller to use in the great outdoors rather than saving it for trips to the mall? Take your tennis shoes to work and walk during your lunch hour?

What we focus on tends to expand. If we zero in on our dislike of exercising, or how we can't find time to do it, or that it really doesn't noticeably reduce our PMS, this will be what pops into our minds when we think about it. But if we focus on making small changes that incorporate more movement into our lives, or making exercise a priority in our schedules each week, or modeling healthy living for our children, our attitude changes from negative to positive, from "can't" to "can," a trait that helps reduce stress.

Instead of being overwhelmed by trying to fit a major new activity in our already overloaded schedules, let's focus on small things that make a big difference. I've noticed that if I get out and walk for 20 minutes on my writing days, my back hurts less at the end of my work session. I've also found that if I take even one lap around the block when PMS starts coloring my world, the jaunt takes my mind off my misery and gives me fresh perspective. (If you have young children and don't have the luxury of heading out without them, take them with you. I know this can be stressful, but at least you're moving and inviting the benefits of exercise into your life and theirs.)

If I don't plan several workouts each week, they don't happen. I sit down with my calendar on Sunday nights and schedule them in. In addition, I'm discovering the renewal that happens when I take advantage of small pockets of time during the week to fit in a brisk walk, a short strength workout, or some sit-ups. My focus is on being more mindful of the value of these short "exercise interludes," working them into my schedule more frequently. Yes, when my schedule gets tight and life gets busy, exercise is usually the first thing to go. Instead of beating myself up about this reality, when I realize exercise has fallen off my agenda, I sit down and schedule my next workout. I encourage you to do the same. You'll be amazed at the difference a little exercise can make. Here are some ways to make exercise fit into your life:

- *Keep a set of hand weights in high-traffic areas of your home.* Do bicep curls, shoulder presses, and tricep exercises while watching TV or helping your kids study for a spelling test. (If you don't know what these exercises entail, look them up online or refer to the next idea.)

- *Treat yourself to a fitness magazine.* Most feature short exercise routines that you can work into your day. I have two articles I tore out of a magazine and laminated for longevity. One is an eight-minute workout to be done in the morning to increase metabolism for the rest of the day, and the other is designed to work my whole body in 15 minutes.

- *Find a workout buddy to walk with or meet at the gym.* Knowing someone is waiting for you is great incentive to get off the couch and get moving. Not only that, exercise seems to go faster when done with a friend. One woman I know shared this about her consistent walking program: "This year I had a friend who agreed to walk with me regularly, and the conversations we've enjoyed have really made the miles go by more quickly."

- *Invest in a workout tape or DVD.* This allows you to work out on your own schedule without leaving home.

- *If you're able, join a gym.* I did! A gym provides a warm place to work out when the weather turns cold. Plus the incentive to "get your money's worth" may help keep you going on those days when exercise is difficult.

- *Involve your children and/or spouse.* Family physician Bryan Albracht met his exercise needs by taking his children along in a running stroller when they were young. As they outgrew the stroller and began riding bikes, he invited them to ride alongside him as he ran. Now he runs with his children—although two of them are now on their school's cross-country team, and Dr. Albracht can barely keep up.

- *Add music.* One woman wrote, "My husband surprised me with an MP3 player for my birthday in May, which really gives me a fun boost for those hot summer months. I wake up early, turn on my 80s tunes, and get my two or three miles in before the kids are up."

- *Experiment.* If aerobics doesn't interest you, but tennis does, join a league or find a tennis partner to play with regularly. If running is boring and you dread it, try swimming or biking. Finding something you enjoy is key to remaining active. Try different activities and stick with what works for you.

- *Mix it up.* Do you get bored easily? If so, it's important not to fall into an exercise rut. Take advantage of the variety offered by seasonal activities such as cross-country skiing and swimming. Alternate aerobic exercise with strength training. Add a dance or martial arts class to your routine to keep things interesting.

- *Pat yourself on the back.* Keep your self-talk encouraging and positive. Rather than criticizing yourself when you don't work out, applaud yourself when you do. One woman bought a package of foil stars and "rewarded" herself after a workout by affixing one on the family calendar each day she exercised. Another mom kept herself going by making an "X" on the family calendar the days she exercised so that she'd have a visual confirmation of her commitment to walking.

- *Multitask.* Stretch while you're watching TV. Do push-ups against the counter while you're waiting for water to boil or for the microwave to finish. Do squats while you brush your teeth.

- *Realize that something is better than nothing when it comes to exercise.* Don't forego exercising just because you don't have a full half hour or hour to do it. When you're pressed for time, shorten your routine. If you can't run three miles, run one. If you can't walk a mile, walk around the block. If you can't make it to the gym, put in an exercise DVD.

Why not make your own list of activities to choose from? Reflect on what has helped inspire and encourage you in the past. What strategies will help you commit to exercise for the long haul? Integrating exercise into your life on a regular basis requires being intentional about making it a priority. If you don't value the benefits of exercise, you won't put it in your schedule. And if it's not in your schedule, you won't likely do it.

I watched with awe recently as my friend Julie got serious about changing old habits. Here's her story.

Having children gave me an excuse to fall back into destructive eating patterns. I was either pregnant, nursing, exhausted, or trying to figure out my new parenting lifestyle, and my food choices reflected my unfocused state of mind. When my youngest daughter was two years old and the weather turned colder, I realized I had one pair of jeans that still fit. I had spent most of the previous year shunning exercise, eating whatever I wanted whenever I wanted, and settling for this heavier, unhealthy me. I wore shapeless clothing and felt frumpy.

In January, I returned to Weight Watchers determined to lose 35 pounds—not at all sure that it would work. But between writing down everything I ate, counting points, attending weekly meetings, and walking 4 to 5 times a week, 40 pounds disappeared over the course of 6 months.

Julie succeeded because she made exercise *and* healthy eating a priority. Notice too that she benefited from writing down everything she ate, something we touched on in the last chapter. She also "acted on what she knows" about herself by signing up for Weight Watchers. Julie confides, "I know I need the regular accountability of stepping on a scale in front of someone else and planning my upcoming food decisions at the meetings."

As Julie continues to see the benefits of her new habits, it will get easier and easier for her to abide by them without having to consciously make decisions as much as she does right now. Initially, changing behavior takes a lot of thought and work. Eventually new habits replace the old ones, making it easier to sustain our changes.

As you consider these chapters on nutrition, stress reduction, and exercise, do you need to develop new habits? That's a great start, but actually creating them can be challenging, especially as the busyness of life presses around us each day. Jerome Daley, a successful life coach, encourages his clients to set "SMART" goals. Consider doing this too. A SMART goal is:

S Specific

M Measurable

A Achievable

R Relevant

T Timely

Here's how this might work. "Exercising more" is a valid goal, but it's not a SMART goal. To make it smart, change the goal this way:

> My goal is to walk [specific type of exercise] for 20 minutes, three times a week [measurable] starting tomorrow and continuing through the end of the year [timely].

Is this goal relevant? Yes, if you want to lose weight or maintain your health. Is it achievable? Yes, if you're fit enough to walk 20 minutes at a time.

How can you benefit from setting a SMART goal or two, either related to exercise or some other facet of PMS management? Write them down. Goals, especially written ones, are the quickest way to go from mindless to meaningful in all areas of our lives.

One last thought. Don't underestimate the value of physical activity as a quick and immediate antidote for PMS symptoms, even if you're not interested in establishing (or reestablishing) an exercise program for yourself. I've often angrily headed out for a walk or run when PMS is at its worst and returned home calm and more able to respond kindly to the needs of my family. Destressing and eating right are important elements in premenstrual self-management, but exercise is probably the quickest and most effective way to respond to out-of-control aspects of PMS "in the moment." Remember this:

- A walk instead of words may keep you from saying something you regret.
- Sit-ups instead of a smack will help protect your children from the sting of your anger.
- Running with your legs instead of your mouth shows respect for your husband.
- Swimming is better than snarling.
- Biking is better than belittling.
- And prayer is the most potent exercise of all.

10

Let's All Just Get on the Titanic

Callie was waiting at the door when Steve arrived. He was 20 minutes late and hadn't called. Normally this wouldn't be a big deal, but Callie had now descended into the depths of PMS and was madder than a hornet. It was bad enough that Steve was late, but not calling sent Callie over the edge. Dinner was sitting on the table getting colder by the minute.

Steve was surprised to see Callie at the door when he walked in. "Hi, babe!" he said, as he leaned in to plant a kiss.

"Don't 'Hi, babe,' me!" Callie said angrily. "Where were you?"

Steve took a step back, and then answered, "Stuck in traffic. There was a semi overturned on Route 6. Traffic was at a standstill until they could get it off the road."

"You could have called," Callie said icily.

"I tried, Callie, but my phone battery was dead. I'm sorry."

"You *always* let your phone battery go dead! What's the use of having a phone if it never works? Last week when I needed milk I couldn't get hold of you because the battery was dead. Why can't you use half your brain and remember to plug it in occasionally? Or do I have to do that for you too?"

Steve moved past Callie, wanting to put her anger behind him. But she wouldn't be denied. She'd spent 20 minutes getting her dander up, and she wanted to see it through.

"Dinner smells good!" Steve exclaimed.

"Thanks to you, it's cold."

"Why don't you call the girls and I'll heat it up," Steve said evenly, refusing to be pulled into a fight.

"You call them. I'm not going to eat with you tonight. I'm sick and tired of being taken advantage of, Steve. I'm not your slave. I'm tired of being the only one who does anything around here. I'm tired of picking up after everyone. I'm tired of doing *your* laundry, cooking *your* meals, and making sure *your* daughters have what they need. You never help and I'm sick of it!"

As Callie listed all the things that made her tired, her voice rose. Steve had heard the same tirade so many times he could practically repeat it word for word. He stayed calm though, realizing that if he didn't the argument would spiral downward quickly, getting more personal and more ugly with every word. He'd made the mistake of letting Callie engage him too often early in their marriage, and many hurtful words had been spoken. He refused to go down that path again, even though she was clearly baiting him.

Steve faced his wife. "Callie, I'm sorry I let you down. I'll take care of feeding the girls. Why don't you take a hot bath or go for a walk or go to Barnes and Noble?"

Callie looked like she had been slapped. "Do you really think you can dismiss me like that?" she hissed through clenched teeth.

"I thought that's what you wanted," Steve responded evenly. "You just told me you aren't going to eat with us. Look, you're angry and disappointed, and I know you don't want the girls to see you like this."

"Fine! I'm *so* out of here! I'm done. You're on your own!" As she turned to head down the hall, large teardrops fell. She wiped them away angrily, determined not to let Steve see her cry. She grabbed her purse and headed out the door. She had no idea where she was going, and it didn't matter. She just wanted to get away.

Callie seethed as she drove. *How dare he! I can't stand him. He makes me crazy. What a jerk! After all I do for him he doesn't even have the courtesy to call. I never should have married him. He obviously doesn't have what it takes to make a relationship work over the long haul.*

Callie got in the turn lane for Barnes and Noble, and then decided to go elsewhere. In addition to running together, Steve and Callie had spent many evenings in the bookstore before the kids came along, paging through books they couldn't afford. The last thing she wanted right now was a reminder of him and the better times they'd shared. Instead, she'd go to the library. She wanted the calming influence of a book in her hand, but she didn't want to be reminded of Steve. She turned the car north and navigated her way into the library lot. She parked the car and then laid her head on the steering wheel and cried angry, hurt tears. So much for the walk she'd planned to suggest after dinner.

Can you identify with Callie's tirade? Unfortunately I can. It has many qualities we may have experienced in ourselves during our PMS years:

- *Being set off by little things.* Steve was 20 minutes late, something that usually doesn't bother Callie. When she's premenstrual, little things become big things.

- *Seeing connections where none exist.* Callie assumes Steve doesn't remember to charge his phone because he doesn't care about her. There's really no connection, but she imagines one because she's under the influence of PMS.

- *Overreacting.* Callie's response to Steve's tardiness is much more intense than called for. Her anger quickly deteriorates into unreasonableness, making it difficult for the couple to resolve the issue without hurting one another.

- *Extreme thinking.* Notice how Callie says that Steve *always* lets his phone battery go dead and *never* helps her. This is "all or nothing" thinking.

- *Belittling.* Callie's words "Why can't you use half your brain" are belittling. They are hurtful and put Steve on the defensive. Imagine what words like that would do to her children if Callie got angry with them.

- *Misinterpreting.* Instead of appreciating Steve's willingness to feed the kids and give her a break, Callie's heightened anger leads her to feeling dismissed rather than loved.

- *Doubting.* What starts as disappointment due to Steve's lateness ends up with Callie questioning her decision to marry him. Again, there's no connection, but Callie's emotions have led her to doubt her decision-making ability (even retroactively). This doubt shakes her self-confidence and lowers her self-esteem.

- *Losing control.* Before the conversation ends, Callie is "talking crazy." What started as a conversation about tardiness becomes a question of whether or not Steve loves her and helps enough around the house. Callie has turned Steve's thoughtlessness in not calling into proof that her marriage was a mistake. Because she's out of control, Callie doesn't stop her runaway words and emotions.

Tirades such as Callie's are part of the downward spiral that can easily occur when we have PMS. Can you imagine what Steve thinks after Callie leaves the house? Probably something like, *Geez! What was that all about? I'm 20 minutes late, and it's the end of the world. And what does being late have to do with how much I help around the house? Where did that come from?*

Usually Callie is loving and forgiving, quick to volunteer to help friends and family members, eager to make a difference in other people's lives, willing to step in and help at the last minute, and shows more patience than most people. Then there's the PMS Callie—the one who overreacts, flies into an instant rage, misinterprets, and is unkind, unfair, and unloving.

I'm sure it's terrifically confusing to live with a PMS wife and mother because little things can set us off and we can be unpredictable. How can we curb this tendency?

Requesting a Life Preserver

If we're serious about changing our PMS responses, we'll chart our symptoms, exercise regularly, watch what we eat, and actively work to reduce stress in our lives. There's another important step we can take so we don't sink our own ship: admit our struggle with PMS to our husbands and ask for their help. This last step, when combined with the others, is powerful, yet it can be terrifically difficult to do. But this idea is what's made the most difference for me and my family.

My husband, Stuart, has been wonderful about stepping in when I need to step out, pitching in when I'm overwhelmed, and extending forgiveness when I've spoken harsh words I later regret.

Sadly, I tried to fight the PMS battle on my own for many years. Now I wish I would have 'fessed up and asked for help much earlier in our marriage. This would have saved us both from a lot of hurt and pain. For many years I was too stubborn to own the problem and unwilling to admit I needed help. The arrival of our children changed the balance. I finally realized that my family's overall health was particularly dependent on my willingness to be honest about what was happening to me each month. What was once manageable became unmanageable. That's when I knew I needed to talk to my husband. Believe it or not, it was a regularly scheduled haircut that helped me finally find the courage to do so.

I don't recall exactly how old my kids were at the time, but it was before they started school. I was an at-home mom, mostly feeling grateful for the privilege. Once a month, though, I doubted my mothering skills, worried about my apparent lack of "mother love," and became short-tempered, which usually resulted in yelling or raising my voice in anger. (Once my daughter looked up at me and said, "You don't have to yell, Mommy. I can hear you.") The winter months were especially difficult as cold set in around November and didn't usually leave for good until April. Combine that with an early Midwestern sunset around 4:30 PM, and we were housebound for what seemed like months at a time.

My husband gets a haircut every four weeks. Every four weeks he'd head to the hair salon on a Friday instead of coming home right after work. The hair appointments became something I dreaded because I was bedraggled by Friday, and the haircuts delayed his arrival home. Worse, they usually fell when I was premenstrual. For years this went on. He had a haircut and was unavailable on the nights I most needed his presence at home. By the time he'd arrive, I was weepy and overwhelmed after a long week of childcare hampered by cold, dark weather and PMS.

I finally worked up the courage to confide in my husband. I was humiliated to admit that something as small as his Friday haircuts made life harrowing for me. I needed them to be on a different night—and preferably a different week. It was a small change I was asking for, but asking was (and still is) difficult for me.

Stuart no longer gets his haircuts on Friday nights. Though it was hard for me to ask him to throw me a life preserver and make the change, it wasn't a big deal for him to change.

Little things become big things when we're premenstrual. That small change made it possible for me to avoid repetitive periods of wrestling with my kids—and PMS—when I knew I was least able to do so successfully.

Though we need the help, understanding, and support of the men in our lives, asking for assistance doesn't guarantee an immediate solution. Some women I surveyed who had shared their PMS struggle with their husbands had this to say about how the men responded:

- It took a long time for him to understand even a little bit.

- He's understanding, but he wants me to work on dealing with the emotions instead of just reacting to situations.

- I think he gets really frustrated and sometimes feels like he has to walk on eggshells.

- He sometimes retreats until my "normal" self returns.

- He's thankful that the PMS me is not the real me. He'll even say, "I figured that had to be it."

- It has taken him years to see this as important.

- He thinks I can just "pray it away."

- He just doesn't get it, but he is supportive.

- He says, "Just because you're going to get your period doesn't mean you can take it out on the rest of us."

As you can see, individual men respond to the PMS challenge differently. Some are willing to step up to the plate, and some refuse to acknowledge it. Others are confused but know that it's essential to periodically shoulder more of the household burden. One man even confided that PMS brought him and his wife closer *after* they addressed the challenge together honestly and head-on. Being united in their response each month deepened their relationship.

Though it would be easier to talk to your husband if you could accurately anticipate his response, the truth is that you won't know how he'll react until you have the conversation. As you can see from the list, for many men acceptance comes with time.

One thing is certain. If you don't let your husband know you need help (and how he can best provide it), you won't get the assistance you need. As much as we'd like them to be, husbands are not mind readers.

If you haven't talked to your husband or asked for his help when you are premenstrual, how does the idea of doing so strike you? Does it make you nervous? Are you thinking there's no way you could acknowledge your PMS challenge to someone else, *especially* your husband? If so, perhaps it would help to see the issue through some men's eyes. In *PMS: Women Tell Women How to Control Premenstrual Syndrome*, these men shared their thoughts.

Mark: She's bright, competent, imaginative, dynamic, and wonderful to be around when she is in her good phase. Then there are those times when, excuse me, she is a real [witch]. She's argumentative, overly emotional, sarcastic, and the last person I want to be around. The differences are really confusing.

Bob: She would put an amazing amount of energy into our fights. Sometimes she really looked like a mad woman. Sorry, but there's no other way to describe it. She would rip clothes out of the closet and throw things. I could see the fear in our kids' eyes. I knew that feeling because I felt it myself. When she'd go crazy like this,

I felt afraid because there was no telling what might happen.

J.D.:   There are times when, no matter what I do, she becomes angry and baits me. It is almost as if she wants to have an argument or a fight. But it doesn't happen all the time. When I started paying attention to the timing, I realized that her mood changed around the time of her period. Then I realized that we were dealing with something on a regular basis.

Jim: PMS chipped away at our relationship. Even though there was a reason for her amazing extremes, craziness, and insulting behavior, it all hurt. Maybe she really couldn't control it, but did she have to be that harsh? She said shocking things. Ninety percent of what she said seemed insane, but 10 percent was true. I was confused with the duplicity of the things she said. I didn't know what to believe.

I would come home at night and say "Hi!" and her response would tell me how the rest of the night would go. If she was in one of her moods, there was no safe place. She would bait me. Every statement would lead to an argument. And the arguments seemed constant, insignificant, and never-ending. I got to the point where I didn't care what the problem was or if there really was one. I couldn't stand it anymore. I thought I was going nuts.[1]

It wasn't easy to read these, was it? Doing so made me wonder what my husband thinks when I'm in the grip of PMS. But it also increased my desire to be proactive about responding to the PMS siren. We may not be able to eliminate PMS, but we know we can influence it.

You and I aren't the only ones who are hurting because of PMS.

As the other adult in our households, our husbands often bear the brunt of our unpredictable and sometimes uncontrollable emotions. They wonder where our sudden fury comes from and what they did to ignite it. Long after we've cooled down, they are still flummoxed by the split-second metamorphosis that turns us from their beloved princess brides into Frankensteins (or worse!) right before their eyes.

Marriage is difficult. But it's even harder when PMS rage, unpredictable behavior, and periodic depression are present. We would be devastated if our husbands treated us like we treat them when we're premenstrual.

Rewriting the Script

How can we change our monthly script from now on? STOP when PMS symptoms start escalating:

S Stop and Silence

T Talk and Tell

O Off to your Oasis

P Ponder and Persevere

Here's how it works. When we sense we're about to respond in a way that's angry or sarcastic, we *stop and silence* ourselves. The more mindful we are that we have PMS (which is why charting is so important), the more we are able to bite our tongues and choose not to say anything rather than chance saying something hurtful. Though this is never easy, the more we practice the art of deliberate silence, the more we'll be able to fall back on it as a valuable coping mechanism during the most difficult phase of our menstrual cycles.

Learning to *stop and silence* takes work. There are two things that might help us master this step. First, as we're learning this skill, we may have to stop ourselves midsentence if we don't stop before beginning to speak. Once I actually interrupted myself. As I began to lose control, I said, "Actually, I don't want to be saying any of this." I surprised myself and my husband by closing my mouth instead of continuing to let words fly. It was a powerful moment. I learned I really could exercise control over what I'd previously thought as "uncontrollable." In fact, the self-knowledge I gained in that passing moment has enabled me to stop and silence myself *before* a tirade begins. Each time I witness the power of choice, I gain more confidence in my ability to STOP.

Second, it may help us to be mindful of a concept introduced by Dr. Emerson Eggerichs in his book *Love & Respect.* He writes:

> But we have made a decision that has changed the course of our marriage for the good…What is this life-changing decision we both have made? I have decided to believe that Sarah does not intend to be disrespectful. Oh, she can get nasty, but that isn't how she feels in her heart. I know she respects who I am deep inside. Sarah has decided to believe that I do not intend to be unloving, though I still hurt her at times with my comments and attitudes. She knows that in my heart I love her deeply and would even die for her.[2]

So what's the life-changing concept? Goodwill. When we choose to believe that our spouses are acting with goodwill as opposed to malice, we can change our whole approach to our relationships. I couldn't believe that such a simple idea could be so revolutionary, but since reading about it, I find myself thinking about it often before I speak. Believing Stuart is not out to "get" me and that he hasn't set out to purposely hurt me has helped me put a brake on a tirade or sarcastic remark before it leaves my mouth. In fact, there have been times when I look like a fish on land gasping for water. I open my mouth to speak, but then close it after considering the concept of goodwill. I still feel the negative PMS feelings and sometimes think nasty thoughts, but I'm less inclined to act on either now. And here's what's really neat: *The more I control my words, the more I want to.* Perhaps the same will be true for you.

After the *stop and silence,* when we're calm enough, *talk and tell.* This means telling our husbands we have PMS and how we're feeling at that moment (depressed, overwhelmed, unusually angry, or what-ever combination of emotions is challenging us), as well as letting them know how they can help (i.e., Would you take the kids to the library after dinner, give the kids their baths, help with homework, etc. The more specific the request, the more likely our husbands will honor them).

When we're talking and telling, I suggest using the "I feel/When/Because" formula for clear communication, followed by a specific request. Simply fill in the blanks:

I feel _____

when _____

because _____.

For example, we might say: "Honey, I *feel* frustrated *when* I'm the only one helping the kids with their homework, especially when I have PMS, *because* life in general overwhelms me at this time of the month. Since I'm most often responsible for helping with homework, would you mind supervising tonight?"

By starting with an "I" statement, we lessen the chance that our spouses will feel defensive when we talk with them. By stating what we feel and why we feel it, we help them understand where we're coming from. By articulating a specific request we help them understand our needs and increase the chance that we'll get the support we need.

Though "I feel/When/Because" is a valuable formula to use any time in our marriages, it's extremely helpful in communicating with our spouses when we're premenstrual so that we can ensure our families' needs are met when we may be unable to meet them. This way, we let our partners know exactly what type of life preserver we need.

Once we've verbalized what we need and are able to take a few minutes, we're off to our *oasis*. This may be the bathtub. Or a backyard swing. Or a coffee shop. Or a guest bedroom. Or outside for a walk around the block (without the kids). Wherever it is, we need to find a place we can retreat to when PMS is about to get the best of us. One woman I know takes her meals to her bedroom and eats alone on her darkest day(s) of the month, leaving her family to enjoy each other's company without tension at the table. (If you've read my book *The Mother Load: How to Meet Your Needs While Caring for Your Family,* you'll know that I sometimes seek refuge in our walk-in closet.)

I love how the dictionary defines "oasis": "a place or period that gives relief from a troubling or chaotic situation." I know of no more "troubling or chaotic situation" than a *mom* with PMS. So we need to go to a place that will quiet our spirits and rejuvenate our souls. Withdrawing is a proven way to refuel so we can keep going.

Finally, when we're in our oasis, *ponder and persevere.* To ponder means to "think deeply," something we must do to conquer the ill-effects of PMS. Think about:

- what works in helping you handle PMS
- what's not working
- who you can turn to when you feel the worst
- how you can involve your family in preventing outbursts each month
- activities to keep your children occupied when you're feeling low
- how you can lighten your load to reduce stress
- things you're doing well in reducing the effects of PMS each month
- whether you're taking care of yourself through exercise, food choices, and sleep
- who you might need to apologize to if you're in the oasis after an unfriendly outburst or altercation

Nothing transforms our lives like the questions we ask—or refuse to ask—ourselves. My greatest personal growth comes when I'm willing to ask—and answer—tough questions about my life. Likewise, my greatest strides in addressing PMS have occurred when I've been willing to sit down and honestly address what's going on and to challenge myself to find workable solutions.

Since we're human, we may make mistakes along the way or lose our commitment or tire of this process. If that happens, we need to forgive ourselves and begin again. It takes perseverance to make positive changes in life. A little change this month may lead to a bigger change next month.

Frankly, I'm still practicing what I've learned about PMS. I find it hard to be silent when I want to scream each month. But now that I've seen I can do it, I have more confidence in other areas. I'm making better food choices. I'm exercising more. I'm apologizing to family members when I speak harsh words instead of looking the other way and pretending it didn't happen. Each month I gain more control. Progress is slow, but it's happening. Little by little hope is replacing despair, and I'm seeing that it's possible to tame the PMS monster.

Perhaps there's another "P" we should add to "STOP" poor behavior when PMS hits: permission. Let's give ourselves permission to be imperfect. Try what we're learning in this book but don't punish ourselves if we don't get it right the first time. Recognize that we're all different, and our approach to PMS should be unique. Capitalize on the ideas that work for us and forget those that don't. Be kind to ourselves when we fail. And give ourselves permission to try again next month. There always will be a "next month" until we reach menopause.

Steve looked up from the computer monitor and saw Callie standing in the doorway of his home office. He'd fed the girls, played the "Pretty Pretty Princess" board game with them, bathed them, and tucked them in. When Callie didn't show up before their bedtime, he assured them she would be home when they woke up in the morning…and hoped it would be true. While he parented solo, he searched his mind for the reason behind his wife's outburst. He couldn't think of a single possibility. Now that she was home, he hoped to get to the bottom of things.

"I'm sorry, Steve," she said quietly.

Steve patted his knee, inviting her to sit down.

"I can't yet. I'm not ready to," responded Callie. "I'm too angry with myself."

"Callie, I'm smart enough to know that something must have set you off. It's not like you to be out of control like that. I'll admit it wasn't my favorite part of the day, but I'm more concerned about what started it rather than the fact that it happened."

"That's the sad part, honey. Nothing set me off...and, at the same time, everything did. It's confusing to me too." Callie continued, "One minute I'm fine, the next I'm losing my mind and having an out-of-body experience. I can feel it happening. I know I'm out of control and need to stop, but I just can't seem to do it. And it's getting worse."

Steve didn't need Callie to tell him things were worsening; he'd noticed. "Callie, when you say it's confusing, what is the 'it' you're talking about? Is it something I'm doing?"

"Oh no! Not at all." Callie crossed over to her husband and took the seat on the knee he'd offered. "It's me. It's PMS—the few days before my period when I'm just not myself. I'm depressed, lethargic, uninterested in anything, afraid I'll lose it with the girls. Sometimes it's so bad that I'm afraid to speak for fear I'll say something horrible. Often I have to cancel play dates. And I'm lucky just to get showered by the time you come home. I hate how I feel on those days, Steve, and I hate how I treated you tonight. Again, I'm so sorry."

"Callster, I love you...despite..."

"Despite? Despite what?"

"Despite what happens to you each month. I know I'm not perfect either. We're a team. If you're having trouble, I've got your back. You can count on me for that," Steve replied. "But I hate being treated like an enemy."

Steve's words melted the ice she'd felt toward him earlier in the evening. As she sat next to him, she felt even more ashamed of her behavior and couldn't believe she'd dared think even for a millisecond that marrying him had been a mistake. Once again, she began to cry. But these were not tears of anger. They were tears of gratitude mixed with sadness that her life now seemed to revolve around squares on a calendar.

"To help, I need to understand what we're up against. Can you help me understand?" Steve asked.

Callie didn't look directly at Steve as she told him about her worsening symptoms and how lonely she felt trying to hide them and handle them on her own. She leaned her head against Steve's chest and could hear his heartbeat as she talked. He listened quietly as his wife shared the specifics of what was happening to her. He heard her mention keeping a calendar so she'd know when it was coming, and she talked about how she was trying to eat better and exercise more. He didn't fully understand how it was all related, but it was clear that she'd been wrestling with this problem on her own for quite a while, and that she was determined to make some changes that would lessen the impact of PMS on the family. He admired her willingness to own up to what was happening.

"Actually, I had already planned to talk to you about this," Callie said. "I've been keeping a list for a couple weeks, recording how you can help me. I wanted to talk to you when I was calm though, not out of control like I was tonight." She was quiet for a moment, and then added, "I have an appointment to talk to the doctor about this later this week."

Though he wasn't sure how, Steve wanted to help. Callie was too emotional and tired to talk more about it tonight, but he made a mental note to ask her about it in the days ahead when the topic was still fresh for both of them. In addition to being concerned about Callie, he was worried about the girls. He needed to know if Callie had better impulse control with them. If she didn't, they would need to do something, but he had no idea what.

Though your husband may not be as kind or as willing to try to understand as Steve was, you owe it to yourself, to him, and to your children to at least approach the subject. His response, in part, will determine your next steps in your effort to cope differently with PMS. Can you count on him for some help? Will you be able to communicate with him and let him know when your worst days are? Is he unsympathetic to your plight and perhaps unwilling to acknowledge it? Remember, it takes some men a while to fully understand and accept the truth about what's happening to you each month. Even if your husband is unable to fully grasp the situation when you first talk about it, he may come around after observing you for a month or two. As you become more able to acknowledge PMS and communicate with him, he may support you in ways you don't anticipate.

Your husband can help watch for changes in your current monthly patterns, which may or may not include more severe symptoms. Knowing that the problem is long-term might also encourage him to rethink his response to your admission that you're struggling. Remember that many men need time to process what you share with them. Let your husband consider the ramifications of living with a PMS wife. His initial response may not be as supportive as you'd like, but hopefully he'll come through in the long run. And it's possible that your husband recognized the PMS symptoms in you long before you did. He may be relieved to have you introduce the subject so that he doesn't have to ignore it or walk on eggshells.

One mom told me that as she feels her PMS symptoms begin each month, she feels doomed. But instead of sinking on the Titanic, let's take steps to get our life preservers on. And your husband may be just the life raft you need each month. Talk to him. Tell him what you need. Let him carry a little extra weight. If he refuses, at least you tried. You can remind him that it would be better to empathize with you rather than be criticized by you.

Perhaps you've already talked about your PMS or your husband's been brave enough to bring the topic up. Maybe you've never been able to talk about it. Either way, the next chapter will be helpful. My husband and I have written letters to your husband. I suggest you read the chapter first. Then, when it's comfortable for you and you have some time alone with your man, invite him to read it. This conversation starter may do a lot of good in your marriage.

Important note: Please don't share the next chapter with your husband when you're premenstrual. (I'm sure you know *why!*) Share it on a day you're feeling good and in control. You need to be focused, honest, upbeat, and able to hear what he has to say—all things that are difficult when PMS strikes.

11

A Letter to Husbands

Thank you for taking the time to read this chapter. It's short so it won't take long. Hopefully it will open the door for an important discussion between you and your wife on how the two of you can work together each month to minimize the effects of premenstrual symptoms (PMS) on your relationship and on your family as a whole.

My name is Mary Byers, and I'm a wife and mother with PMS. I hate it. I kept silent about it for too long, which was difficult on my husband and marriage. Since your wife is sharing this with you, you probably can relate. As you've noticed your wife being very emotional and unpredictable during "that time of the month," you probably decided it was dangerous for you to say anything. To keep the peace, you may have chosen to say nothing at all.

PMS is a difficult subject for wives to bring up. But your wife has chosen to share this chapter with you. She wants you to know she's working to change how her PMS symptoms affect you and your family each month. She knows that living with her can seem like living with Dr. Jekyll and Mrs. Hyde sometimes. That's why she's reading this book—to proactively develop a plan that will head off and minimize the negative results of PMS.

Finding a way for the two of you to respond together to this issue will improve your marriage. One man I interviewed shared, "If women really grasp this and men learn how to respond, it's pretty neat."

I've asked my husband, Stuart, to share his experiences and some ideas he has about how to create your own PMS plan to negotiate and help your wife through the few days of PMS every month.

Plan, Maneuver, Sympathize

Dear Fellow PMS Survivor,

I hid my apprehension when my wife asked me to write this chapter, much as I did when my boss asked me to write a 180-degree appraisal. Who came up with that lame idea anyway? Ask your employee, whose livelihood depends on your good graces, to write your appraisal. Brilliant! I bet all of corporate America received a very realistic view of how everyone was performing.

When my other half invited me to contribute to this book I felt like I was asked to not only write my own death warrant, but to sign it as well. But then I thought back to the many "couples" books my wife and I have shared in the past, and how I thought that the male writers must be from a different planet. I felt those guys were playing it safe to appease either their spouses or their intended audience. They were honest, but they were being typically male and weren't going to jeopardize their marital bliss by telling it like it is. I decided that since I agreed to share my thoughts on this potentially dangerous subject, I wasn't going to sugarcoat it. (I did request that Mary not review this when she had PMS!)

I once had a female boss who was normally a very easy person to work for. About my third month working for her, I noticed that some days she just wasn't her usual kind self. I commented on that to a female coworker, who quickly pointed out that it was probably PMS. Having heard of this affliction, and also thinking it might be funny, I flipped my calendar forward four weeks and made a note. A month later I noted my boss' behavior. Sure enough, no smiles. Short conversations. Too serious. She had PMS all right. I tracked her for quite some time to our mutual benefit.

I've always been pretty good about meeting my scheduled obligations. I enjoy routine and order. I once had a wristwatch that allowed me to schedule events and a timer would go off to remind me to take action. I used it even for regular monthly stuff. Mortgage payments, utility bills, credit card bills, and haircuts were all on there. But what wasn't on there? You guessed it. The most important person in my life, in her most difficult days, fell off my radar. Even though I felt the brunt of this monthly event, I didn't plan for it. So here is the first tip: *Plan for "Aunt Menny" to visit once a month.* Some visits may be okay or they may all be rough, but you can count on her to visit each month like clockwork.

For the five percent of you who have that near-perfect relationship, you can enhance it further by sitting down with your wife and spending some quality time holding hands and plotting out the next year regarding the monthly event. Or, if you're one of those who just want to improve your relationship with your spouse, you can share with her (when she is in a good mood), that you want to be more sympathetic to her situation and need her assistance in noting her dark days. (Then again, if you're a typical guy, you don't want to risk starting any conflict and can just take note of the day when she seems upset over something trivial, she picks a fight over something trivial, or she notes that you treat her as something trivial, and secretly note that day somewhere and begin your stealth tracking. You're gonna suffer anyway. You might as well know it's coming.) Anticipation of those difficult days is the key to performing the next step in helping you and your wife weather difficult times.

> Plan for the monthly PMS symptoms.

When you suspect or are aware that your wife is going to morph into someone you don't remember meeting, you have a greater chance to either maneuver her or yourself into a better position to deal with it. I recommend starting a day before she's premenstrual so she will be more receptive to your kind works than she is after "the transformation" takes place.

You probably already know that the simplest loving gestures from us Neanderthals is deeply appreciated more than we can even begin to understand. All you need to do is:

- complete a simple chore without being asked
- rub her shoulders and then walk away (walking away with a smile is the hard part, and it will leave her wondering)
- give her a greeting card with a complete sentence of kindness before your signature
- send her out for some self-time
- offer to stop and pick up dinner on your way home

This preemptive strike will give your wife additional strength before the demons arrive. On alternate months, you should change your approach, just to keep it fresh. This might include:

- staying late at work to finish a project (but let her know you'll be late)
- heading to the home-improvement store for some lengthy browsing
- going to visit your mother
- volunteering at a homeless shelter
- grabbing the kids and heading out of the house so she can have time alone (but always let her know where you are!)

Making yourself scarce with a valid excuse will spare you the arrow in your heart and soul.

Last, but most important: Sympathize with your woman. Just as man has been cursed with an insatiable sexual appetite, many women have been cursed with monthly mental and physical illness. Cruel but true. This natural occurrence can't be helped by your spousal unit. The poor thing knows it's coming and usually knows when it's upon her, and she truly struggles with it. This is when she is at her worst, and you often *appear* at your worst as well. This is when any negative little habit or response from you really gets noticed. So

> Take steps to help your wife be positive, arrange alternative plans, or give her alone time.

when you hear those dreaded words "We need to talk," that is your cue that you need to *listen*.

I know, I know. You want to defend yourself or solve the dilemma, but that is not what is required from you. Remember, she is temporarily chemically unbalanced. All you need to do is suck it up and hear her out. Pay attention for as long as you can, and then wait another two minutes, all the while staring directly into her eyes while counting down those 120 seconds. Gently say, "I hear you" and "I love you." I know these four minutes will seem like an eternity, and that is completely normal. You will get used to it and possibly even excel at it. To help reinforce this, try to imagine there is an ice pick hidden under the mattress on your wife's side of the bed with your name on it. That should help you maintain eye contact and maybe even add a little head nodding so she knows she has your attention. Thankfully your "old wife" will be back tomorrow or the next day. Right now you just want the both of you to survive this brief time period without scars.

> Sympathize with your woman.

I remember taking my wedding vows and, at that young age, thinking, *In sickness and in health might entail bringing her a box of tissues when she caught a cold.* That vow really meant I would be with her *every single day of the month,* not just the best three weeks. We all know that our wives would do anything for us to help us through our rough days—if we let her know about them. Well, your wife will let you know one way or another about hers, and if you want to show how much you truly love her, you'll make the effort to *plan, maneuver,* and *sympathize* with her—our own kind of PMS—during her difficult days.

Sincerely,

Stuart Byers

Coping Techniques from Mary

Well, guys, there you have it, my husband's coping techniques for dealing with me on my bad days. Honestly, I didn't even know he had any until I signed a contract to write this book. He's a smart man, my Stuart. Smart because he has a plan and because he never told me about it until now.

Seriously, two things to avoid are patronizing your wife when she's experiencing PMS and asking if it's "that time of the month" in response to a situation or conversation. Those two things will cause even the mildest case of PMS to turn into a survival issue—possibly yours!

Here's the crazy thing about PMS: Women who suffer from it often know it's coming, *but sometimes we're still surprised when it happens.* Unbelievable, I know. How can someone who struggles with the same thing month after month after month be surprised when it arrives? I'll tell you. We're busy. We're distracted. We're focused on our jobs and meeting your needs as well as those of our sweet, wonderful children. And the emotions we experience each month are so overwhelming and debilitating that we don't always connect the dots. Scarier still, sometimes we can connect the dots and we know it's happening, but *we still have to fight to stop the negative behavior.* Your wife is reading this book because she wants the future to be different from the past. She wants to understand what's happening to her and what she can do to change it or minimize the impact of PMS.

The bad news is there is no magical answer. The good news is that she's learning a lot of coping techniques that she can use to create a personalized approach to managing her PMS. I believe you'll see changes over the next several months. One of the biggest may be that she will ask for your specific help instead of struggling alone during her difficult times. When she does, I hope you'll pitch in. Please be positive and affirming because she cares enough about you and your children to deal with this issue. Encourage her when she stumbles and continue to do your best to love her when she seems unlovable.

That's the paradox of family life: Humans need love *especially when they're hurting*. You'll gain many points with your wife if you remain calm in the face of her overreactions, be patient when she's impatient, and steady when she's unsteady. And guys, don't talk about this very personal situation in social settings or openly "blame" PMS for a wife's response to something. Disaster will follow.

The three top things doctors recommend to reduce PMS symptoms are exercise, good nutrition, and stress reduction. You might offer to watch the kids so your wife can take a walk, go for a run, or head to the gym. Look for ways you can reduce her stress when she's premenstrual. Stress magnifies PMS symptoms. She may need help even with the day-to-day chores she normally handles with no problem. She may not ask, so be proactive.

Although I've come a long way in coming to terms with warning my husband that "Black Tuesday" (our code for PMS) is coming, it's still difficult for me to admit I'm less than the perfect wife and mother. It's still hard for me to ask for help even when I know I need it. Stuart blesses me by using these phrases when I have PMS. They might be helpful in your marriage too:

- "How can I help you?"
- "Why don't you take a break and let me clean up the dinner dishes?"
- "I know you've had a hard day. Why don't you let me get the kids to bed?"
- "I'd be happy to cover homework duty tonight."
- "How about if I stop and pick up dinner on the way home?"
- "The kids and I would like some time together. Why don't you take the night off?" (Okay, I haven't actually heard this one yet, but I'd like to. I can always hope, right?)

When I hear these phrases, I'm hearing, "I love you!" They offer support without being or appearing condescending. (Whatever you do, don't start any of these phrases with "Because it's that time of the month…"! Your health may be in jeopardy.

Are you wondering why *you* are being asked to accommodate your wife since *she's* the one with the problem? PMS is a *family* problem. When you married, you and your wife wove the threads of your lives together. When you added children to the mix, the quilt became even more warm, colorful, and complex. As wonderful as kids are, you know they increase stress…and stress magnifies PMS. And since PMS often worsens as women age, the problem may get worse before it gets better.

You do have a choice. You can be her rock when she's in the throes of PMS or you can stand aside, hoping to avoid any barbs hurled your way. Though I haven't walked in your shoes and don't know how bad it is for you, I can tell you this: Relationships forged in fire develop a beautiful finish that's not found on unrefined gold or silver. You will bless your wife and your marriage with your unselfishness. And your entire family will benefit.

Thanks for taking the time to read this. I hope you and your wife will take on managing PMS together in a positive, proactive way. She doesn't like what's happening to her each month any more than you do. If you can talk about it (when she's not premenstrual, of course) and develop a coping plan together, you'll find your relationship will become deeper and stronger.

12

To Medicate or Not

Callie waited in the reception area of her doctor's office, the sting of last night's fight still fresh in her mind. She regretted lashing out at Steve just because he was 20 minutes late—and it was something he couldn't avoid. Last year at her checkup she asked her gynecologist about taking antidepressants to help deal with PMS symptoms after reading about the practice in a magazine. She took a three-month sample home but never opened it, thinking she should be able to "beat" PMS on her own. Eventually she tossed the pills. Now she wished she'd tried them. Nothing could be worse than the apathy she felt right now combined with the overreactiveness that caused her to create such a scene last night. She didn't understand what was happening. She remembered a postcard she saw recently that said "PMS: Good Girls Gone Bad." It certainly applied to her.

"Callie O'Keefe," called a grumpy, stern-looking nurse. Callie rose from her chair and followed the woman down the hall. She wondered if the nurse had PMS.

As she waited in the exam room, she thought about Steve and the girls. They were her most precious assets, yet she didn't always treat them like the treasures they were. What was happening to her?

After knocking, Dr. Megan Ray opened the door and peered in. She had been Callie's gynecologist since her first female exam in her late teens and had delivered Amber and Jessica. She smiled at Callie. "How's it going, young lady?"

"So so," Callie replied. "How are you?"

"Doing okay," Dr. Ray replied as she entered the room and sat down.

"How's the empty nest?" Callie asked.

"Wow! You have a good memory, Callie. We do have an empty nest. And

I hate to admit it, but it's kind of nice. The phone doesn't ring incessantly, I don't have to wake up to make sure our youngest made curfew, and I only do laundry every two or three days!"

The two women talked briefly about their kids and being parents.

"Was child-rearing difficult for you?" Callie asked.

"Of course it was. There's nothing easy about it. Why do you ask?"

"I'm really struggling," confided Callie. "I don't have the joy other moms seem to have. I cry a lot. I'm insecure. And one week out of the month I'm an angry mess."

"How long has this been going on?" Dr. Ray asked in a gentle voice.

Callie fingered her hair as she spoke. "Last year when I came in you gave me samples of antidepressants. At the time I was fighting overwhelming sadness. Since then it's gotten worse. In addition to the sadness, I've become a real witch. I yell. I scream. I'm impatient and yet apathetic. I don't understand what's happening to me, but I know I need to do something about it. It's affecting my marriage and my confidence as a mom. At the suggestion of a friend, I've been writing down what I've been experiencing for the past couple of months. I have it with me if you'd like to see it."

"Definitely."

Callie offered her charts to Dr. Ray. Though they were rough, they did a good job providing a snapshot of the last three months.

"How did the antidepressants work?" Dr. Ray asked as she studied the charts.

"I didn't take them," Callie admitted. "I felt I should be able to handle things on my own, and I didn't like the idea of taking medication daily. Now, though, I can see I need help, and I'm willing to try again if you agree."

"Sure, Callie. But I need to ask you a few questions before we decide what's best."

Callie's willingness to talk to her health-care provider shows she is serious about finding a solution for her haywire emotions. She's taking a whole-life approach to the problem by charting her symptoms to know when to expect the mood swings each month, exercising more, and paying attention to what she eats. She is also doing what she can to reduce stress and has confided in her husband. Yet her symptoms continue to be disruptive. Now, she and her doctor will decide if medicine should be added to her PMS-busting regimen.

After you've implemented what we've talked about so far and a couple of months have passed, evaluate where you are. You may find that the changes you've experienced could use some enhancement. If that's the case, you may want to consider adding medication to your routine.

Women's reactions to the idea of medicating for PMS vary widely. The focus group I conducted seemed to be evenly split on the topic. Some women said "No way!" while others said "Bring it on! The sooner the better." Though the focus group wasn't a statistically randomized sample, I believe it reveals typical responses to the idea of medication. Some women have no qualms about taking it while others will do so only as a last resort. What is your attitude about this approach? If you have qualms, please read through this chapter anyway. You'll find it informative and practical.

Dr. Bryan Albracht, a family physician in Springfield, Illinois, suggests considering the following when making a decision about whether to take medication for PMS symptoms:

- Is PMS causing problems in your daily life?
- Have you tried everything else without success?
- Are your symptoms getting worse?
- Has a family member confronted you about "needing help"?

If you answered yes to one or more of these questions, why not explore the possibility of a prescription to help with the severity of your symptoms? Here's what one mom wrote about her decision to begin taking an antidepressant:

> The bottom line for me is that I feel better. My anxiety is less and my PMS is better. I will continue to take it as

long as necessary, unless problems arise from it…That said, my PMS is not gone. I still have symptoms, but they're not as bad as they used to be. I strongly encourage any woman who really struggles with raging PMS to check into medications. It's worth it! I now feel in control of my PMS instead of having my PMS control me…

Specifically, my emotions are less volatile. I'm not as teary or easily upset, and I'm more rational. However, I still have mood swings, though they're much milder and easier to recognize, which makes them easier to deal with. Call it PMS Lite! Yet the cravings for starchy foods and chocolate are still there in force. (But it's nothing that a pound of chicken tettrazini and M&M's can't handle!)

Medication doesn't magically make PMS symptoms disappear, but it can reduce the severity and make the symptoms more manageable. If you talk to your doctor about PMS, he or she will ask a series of questions designed to determine if you're dealing solely with premenstrual syndrome or PMS augmented by clinical depression and/or anxiety. It's important for your physician to take the time to determine what's truly going on because many people who've been diagnosed with depression have symptoms of anxiety, which may need to be treated separately. Your health-care provider will also want to be sure you aren't experiencing symptoms indicative of another condition. The following mimic PMS:

- fibrocystic breast changes
- endometriosis (pain and cramping)
- pelvic inflammatory disease
- dysmenorrhea (cramps secondary to other factors)
- thyroid disorders
- endocrine disorders (such as abnormal adrenal function)
- clinical depression

- menopause
- birth-control pill side effects
- eating disorders[1]

Once your physician has ruled out another illness, he or she will decide which medication is best for you. The medicine prescribed for PMS addresses low serotonin or other neurotransmitters. These chemicals allow nerve cells to communicate with one another. When serotonin is at an ideal level, you feel mellow and relaxed, hopeful and optimistic. You have a sense of being at peace with life. You are creative, thoughtful, and focused. Low serotonin levels can result in feeling depressed, having a short attention span, feeling "blocked" or scattered, acting impulsively, feeling suicidal, and craving sweets and simple carbohydrates to quickly increase the serotonin level, but this can also lead to wild swings in blood sugar as noted earlier.[2]

Generally, there are three classes of medicine your physician might prescribe to address serotonin issues: selective serotonin reuptake inhibitors (SSRIs), trycyclics (TCAs), and monamine oxidase inhibitors (MAOIs). The last group is the least popular due to potentially serious side effects and is prescribed only for those who don't respond to the other classes.

As serotonin is released from one nerve cell and passed to another, some of it is reabsorbed by the first nerve cell. SSRIs block the reabsorption, resulting in an increase in the amount of serotonin available.

Some SSRIs can be taken for two weeks out of the month during the premenstrual phase (starting two weeks *after* the day your period begins) rather than daily for help with PMS symptoms. If you prefer not to take medication daily, this option is worth exploring. The cost is also less since you only take pills for two weeks each month. If you use an SSRI for 10 to 14 days of your cycle, you will probably experience an improvement in energy, motivation, and decreased carbohydrate cravings. This regimen usually does not address anxiety issues.

Another class of antidepressants is called "tricyclics," so-named because of the shape of the drug's three-ring antihistaminic chemical structure. These antidepressants work by helping norepinephrine and serotonin, two neurotransmitters in the brain, work more effectively. This class of antidepressants is older than the SSRIs. Due to the number of side effects of tricyclics, patients usually start on an SSRI and move to a tricyclic only if depression or PMS symptoms don't respond to other drugs.

Another older class of antidepressants are monoamine oxidase inhibitors (MAOIs):

> Once the brain's three neurotransmitters, known as mono-amines (serotonin, norepinephrine, and dopamine), have played their part in sending messages in the brain, they get burned up by a protein in the brain called monoamine oxi-dase, a liver and brain enzyme. MAOIs work by blocking this cleanup activity. When the excess neurotransmitters don't get destroyed, they start piling up in the brain. And since depression is associated with low levels of these mono-amines, it's not surprising that increasing the monoamines ease depressive symptoms.[3]

MAO inhibitors have been known to cause sudden, sometimes fatal increases in blood pressure so they are used for individuals who don't respond to any other medication.

Be aware that most, if not all, antidepressants have side effects that may include nausea, increased appetite and weight gain, sexual side effects, fatigue and drowsiness, insomnia, dry mouth, blurred vision, constipation, dizziness, and agitation, restlessness, and/or anxiety. Though many of these side effects last only a few weeks and then go away on their own, some remain. Only you and your doctor can decide if the benefits gained outweigh potential side effects.

If one medication doesn't work, your health-care provider may add a second drug designed to work in tandem with the first. In some cases, finding the combination that's effective for you may take several months. Be patient. You can help the process by keeping a daily log of how you feel. As with your symptoms chart, the more specific your medication log is, the more effective it will be in helping you and your doctor make informed choices.

If the idea of taking an antidepressant doesn't appeal to you, another option is birth control pills, which may even out your hormone levels throughout your cycle. Like other medicines, birth control pills may have side effects to consider. Though this option doesn't help all women, your physician can help you determine if it might be right for you.

Should you decide to consider medication, bring your symptom chart to your appointment. You may also want to prepare a list of questions in preparation for your appointment. If your list is long, consider scheduling a double appointment so your doctor isn't hurried during your visit. Take two copies of your questions—one for you and one for your doctor. You might check to see if e-mailing your list to the doctor a few days before your appointment is an option. This way you and your doctor can move through your questions as efficiently as possible (and so your physician knows how many questions you have).

Your symptom chart and personal questions will provide the main agenda for your medical visit, but it's helpful to have a list of the current medications you're taking (including dosage). Include any supplements and herbal alternatives you use. Make sure your doctor has an updated medical history. Mention any major life changes (such as a divorce or death in the family) that may be affecting your mood or ability to concentrate. Another time-saving and practical help for your doctor is taking along the answers to these questions:

1. How old were you when you began menstruating?

2. When was the first day of your last period?

3. How many days does your period usually last?

4. How many days are in your cycle (how many days between the start of one period and the next)?

5. How would you describe your menstrual flow (light, medium, heavy, extra heavy)?

6. Are you experiencing any other problems with your menstrual cycle?

7. Do you eat a balanced diet?

8. Do you exercise regularly? If so, what do you do and how often do you do it?

9. Are you on any prescription medications or taking any supplements?

10. Is there a family history of cancer, diabetes, high blood pressure, heart disease?

11. Are you getting adequate sleep?

12. Have you had any major illnesses?

13. Do the symptoms you've charted dissipate with the start of your period?

14. Are your symptoms consistent month to month?

15. Are your symptoms seriously disrupting your life? If so, how?

16. What symptoms bother you the most?

17. Has anything happened in your life recently that has increased your stress level?

When combined with a complete health history, a list of current prescriptions, and your chart, your doctor will likely have what he or she needs to determine if medication will help—and what type might be the most effective in addressing your particular concerns.

If you and your doctor decide that an antidepressant would be helpful, be prepared to give the medicine time to stabilize serotonin levels and give you a true picture of how well they work for you. (We'll discuss other, natural ways to aid this effort in the next chapter.) Plan on four to six weeks before you see any major improvement; in most cases, after 10 weeks you'll realize the full benefit and any side effects still present will likely remain. (In rare cases it may take 12 to 14 weeks to achieve the full effects of an antidepressant.)[4] Give the drugs adequate time to work before deciding whether or not to keep them as part of your therapy.

After using an antidepressant to stabilize neurotransmitters, some women eventually discontinue their prescription. However, Dr. Albracht cautions that discontinuation should be done in cooperation with your physician because you need to *taper* off the medicine rather than quit cold turkey. This allows your body to adjust as necessary. Dr. Albracht estimates that 30 percent of his patients who begin taking antidepressants are able to discontinue or decrease the prescription at some point. Another 30 percent discontinue, then choose to start again due to the return of their symptoms. And 30 percent remain on medication permanently.

If you're one of the many women who have qualms about medication, consider what Dr. Albracht says:

> If you came to me and we did your lab work and your blood sugar was 500…Or let's say it's your child…you wouldn't think twice about treating medically for diabetes because if you don't, there are horrible ramifications. The body is not producing enough insulin necessary to control the blood sugar…The same thing happens with the neurotransmitters in the brain if you're not producing enough serotonin…Medicine is simply another way we can treat it.

At one time there was a stigma about Christians and antidepressants. Dr. Albracht calls this the "Christian trap," when we believe God should provide physical and emotional relief Himself rather than having us rely on medicine. Says Dr. Albracht, "I've seen miracles. But God also gave us the medical knowledge to treat…and this (PMS) is a medical problem."

As you consider whether or not medicine is appropriate in your situation, it might be helpful to consider this from Dr. Eaker, who encourages us to look at how Jesus healed:

[Jesus] didn't heal the same way every time. Sometimes he spoke words, sometimes he touched. Sometimes he prayed, sometimes he was long distance. Sometimes he used spit. Sometimes he used mud. He used many tools to heal. I believe God uses a number of different tools to heal. To limit those tools, in essence, is really to limit God. He provides things like medication, like antidepressants…as tools for healing…All healing comes from God, but it comes through different pathways.

If you've tried the suggestions in previous chapters and aren't seeing a marked improvement in your symptoms, medicine may be an option. Talk to your physician. Dosages can be set low, the medicine doesn't always have to be taken daily, and side effects are often very manageable. If you have friends or family members who are currently benefiting from pharmaceutical therapy, ask them how they've been helped. I found it helpful when I learned that some PMS moms I know feel they have improved greatly from taking medication. The more I learned about how these women have been helped—and the benefits for their families—the less resistant I became.

My research revealed that the best approach to PMS requires a multipronged response that addresses the emotional and physical aspects of PMS. The results are interrelated: When you're feeling better physically, you feel better emotionally. And when you feel better emotionally, you're more likely to be physically active.

The wisest PMS solution entails identifying what needs to change in your life, making the easiest changes first, and gradually moving to the more difficult ones. If these don't produce the results you and your family need, or you don't feel you have the luxury of time to try them, consult with your physician. In addition to determining if medication is an option, you might consider a natural approach.

The Serotonin and Supplement Mystery

Dr. Ray returned with a prescription for antidepressants. She handed it to Callie, and then rolled her stool back and studied her patient. "Let's talk about some other options you have in addition to medication."

"Okay," responded Callie.

"I suspect that some of your symptoms are caused by low serotonin, Callie. That's one of the neurotransmitters that allows your nerve cells to communicate with one another. The serotonin system is the largest single system in your brain, and it influences a wide range of functions, from movement to mood. Antidepressants are one way to increase serotonin, but there are others as well."

Callie reached for her purse and grabbed a small spiral notebook her daughter Abby had given her for Christmas. It had "I love you mummy" written on it, which Callie thought was adorable. She planned to keep the notebook even after the pages were gone due to Abby's youthful misspelling of "mommy."

"Okay, I'm ready," Callie said. "I'm taking notes so I won't forget."

"First, think about 'three S's and an E,'" Dr. Ray noted. "That stands for sleep, sunlight, sex, and exercise. All four of these *increase* serotonin."

Callie repeated the items as she hastily jotted them down.

"Caffeine, alcohol, and stress *lower* serotonin. I encourage you to increase the amount of sleep, sunlight, sex, and exercise you get while decreasing the amount of stress, caffeine, and alcohol."

"How important are these?"

"Well, 30 minutes of aerobic exercise is approximately the equivalent of 20 milligrams of Prozac, and I've just started you on a dosage of 10 milligrams. That tells you how powerful exercise is. In fact, I have another patient who was in yesterday who told me that she'd stopped walking for several months due to a family crisis. She didn't realize how negatively it was affecting her until she started walking again and noticed the improvement in her mood and coping ability. That's the serotonin working. The three S's and an E increase serotonin, are absolutely free, and don't have any side effects," Dr. Ray observed.

"Should I try those before I try the antidepressant?"

"It's up to you, Callie. But since PMS has disrupted your life enough that you made a special trip to see me, and since you're concerned about how it's affecting your mothering, I suggest you try the medicine while simultaneously paying close attention to these other things. It's possible that after we get your serotonin levels evened out, we'll be able to take you off the medicine."

"How long will that take?"

"Usually six to nine months. In fact, you might not see a noticeable change for a month or two. I know it sounds like a long time, but there are no magical answers." Dr. Ray's voice softened. "I do believe you'll see considerable improvement, Callie. PMS is treatable, and you're doing the right things to address this challenge in your life."

"Thanks, Dr. Ray. For the first time in a long time I actually believe I can get this monkey off my back. Thanks for being so sympathetic and taking my concerns seriously. I feel less alone and like I'm not imagining what's happening or losing my mind."

Dr. Ray rose from her stool. "Say hi to those beautiful little girls for me, will you? Also, check in with me in a month and let me know how things are going."

"Sure," Callie agreed, realizing that to report back, she'd have to at least give something a try this time around.

In addition to exercise, good nutrition, minimizing stress, and enlisting help, Callie is learning other valuable PMS management tips. Though the number of considerations in keeping PMS at bay may seem overwhelming at first, everything you've heard about good health in general is also true for replenishing serotonin levels:

- limit or avoid caffeine
- get adequate sleep
- exercise 20 to 30 minutes, five days a week
- reduce stress any way possible
- get 20 minutes of sunlight daily when feasible (but don't burn!)
- limit alcohol intake
- have sex frequently

Okay, I admit that I haven't previously heard this last point mentioned as something that promotes health, but it does increase serotonin, and therefore is a specific way to respond to PMS symptoms. I can hear it now: Men all across America saying, "Honey, may I help with your PMS?" The irony is that often when we have PMS, we have no interest in sex. While it might be too much to suggest the possibility of spontaneous sex when you have PMS, maybe there's value in scheduling it (something busy couples often have to do, and which therapists often recommend). One woman confided, "The more I have sex, the more I want it." She schedules it at least once a week, knowing that a scheduled encounter often leads to an unscheduled one later in the week. Another woman shared that her husband also gets grumpy when she's premenstrual because he knows "there's no chance for intimacy during that time."

It's complicated enough to be a mom with PMS, but even more complicated to be a married woman with PMS. Sometimes bed is the very best refuge from premenstrual syndrome. You can curl up with a good book, wrap a heating pad around a cramping abdomen, or avoid giving an unwanted tirade by sleeping. Yet men often see bed as a playground. Needless to say, these visions are incompatible, requiring a meeting of the minds. If you need your space, be sure to communicate this verbally to your spouse so that you're not surprised with an amorous advance when you're least willing and/or able to respond.

Sleep Needs

In the chapter on reducing stress, we learned that 52 percent of women polled responded that sleep is one of the first things they sacrifice when they are pressed for time. Since we know sleep increases serotonin, skimping on it really isn't a great option for those of us who suffer from PMS. Our children also need to get enough sleep when we're premenstrual since well-rested kids are less likely to act up. Many people underestimate their sleep needs. Here's what you and your family need:[1]

How Much Sleep Do You Really Need?

Age	*Sleep Needs*
Newborns (1-2 months)	10.5-18 hours
Infants (3-11 months)	9-12 hours during night and 30-minute to two-hour naps, one to four times a day
Toddlers (1-3 years)	12-14 hours
Preschoolers (3-5 years)	11-13 hours
School-aged children (5-12 years)	10-11 hours
Teens (11-17)	8.5-9.25 hours
Adults	7-9 hours

There is a reason sleep deprivation is used as a form of torture! Think about it: Lack of sleep leads to problems concentrating, daytime sleepiness, increased accidents, poor performance on the job and in school, and, possibly, sickness and weight gain. Fatigue feeds crankiness, short-temperedness, and impatience. It's a mother's worst enemy. Yet many of us limit our sleep time. And most of us assume that's "just the way it is," and we have little choice. But we do have control! We're just not always willing to exercise it. We don't want to say no to more projects and activities for ourselves and our families. We don't enforce our children's bedtimes so that we too can get to sleep at a decent hour. We haven't taught our children to sleep in their own beds so we won't experience the sleep interruption that's inevitable with a tossing toddler. Though most adults require between 7 and 9 hours of sleep each night, most women between 30 and 60 sleep less than 7 hours during the work week.[2] Are you shortchanging yourself?

Though the quantity and quality of your sleep is important all month long, when you're premenstrual you may experience some of these sleep-related challenges: insomnia (difficulty falling asleep, staying asleep, waking up too early, unrefreshed sleep), hypersomnia (sleeping too much), and daytime sleepiness.[3] Adequate sleep encourages serotonin production; lack of sleep lowers serotonin. Since we know serotonin is a major mood enhancer, we need to take steps to allow healthy sleep patterns. In addition to getting a sufficient amount, the National Sleep Foundation offers these tips for good sleep:

- avoid caffeine (coffee, tea, soft drinks, chocolate) and nicotine (cigarettes, tobacco products) close to bedtime
- avoid alcohol as it can lead to disrupted sleep
- exercise regularly, but complete your workout at least three hours before bedtime
- establish a regular relaxing, not alerting, bedtime routine (e.g., taking a bath or relaxing in a hot tub)
- create a sleep-conducive environment that is dark, quiet, cool, and comfortable.[4]

If any of your children currently are experiencing sleep problems, you might apply these suggestions to them as well. Sleep problems are often interrelated. If your kids aren't sleeping well, you probably aren't either.

Sunlight

I live in the Midwest. In the winter it's not unusual to go days and days without seeing sunshine. In fact, one year an editor I worked with and I kept track of the number of days without the sun. We counted 21 days before it peeked out from behind the clouds! It wasn't surprising that my mood was low during that time. I envy those of you who live in sunnier states.

Lack of sunshine can cause a drop in serotonin. Though too much exposure to the sun can be unhealthy, just minutes a day can help keep you balanced. Here are some ideas to help you capture what you can of the sunshine's beneficial rays:

- sit close to bright windows while at home or in the office
- make your home as sunny and bright as possible by opening blinds and trimming tree branches that block sunlight
- get outdoors on sunny days to take a walk, read a book, or enjoy a picnic lunch
- look straight ahead rather than down at the ground when you walk. This can more than double the amount of light that enters your eyes, the primary way your body senses light (and absorbs vitamin D)
- install the brightest full-spectrum light bulbs your lamps will allow
- move your workout outside whenever possible. Biking, running, walking, and swimming all enable you to take advantage of the benefits of sunshine. (Allow 10 to 20 minutes of safe exposure to sunlight, and then apply sunscreen.)

Caffeine As Coconspirator

Too much caffeine and/or alcohol interferes with sleep. Since lack of sleep leads to fatigue, we often seek a caffeine jolt to get us going in the morning—and the unhealthy cycle starts all over. Here's what Dr. Marcelle Pick has to say about caffeine addiction:

> My biggest concerns for most women with chronic caffeine use are increased anxiety, insomnia, inflammation, and

adrenal burn-out. Symptoms of fatigue, PMS, sleepless-
ness, and breast tenderness are exacerbated by caffeine use.
Caffeine distances you from your natural energy cycles,
tricking your body into a constant state of alert. This ultimately makes you more tired. If you use caffeine to cope
with stress, you can't ignore the fact that your solution may
be part of the problem.[5]

Symptoms of PMS are exacerbated by caffeine use. How much are
you consuming daily? An average 8-ounce cup of *generic* brewed coffee
has 80 to 133 milligrams (mg). A typical diet soda has between 36
and 47 mg and regular soda ranges from 35 to 54 mg, depending on
the brand. (Moderate caffeine consumption is considered to be around
250 milligrams per day.) If you'd like to calculate how much you're
consuming each day, go to http://www.cspinet.org/reports/caffeine.
pdf or http://www.energyfiend.com/the-caffeine-database.

If your calculations reveal that caffeine may be a problem for you,
consider reducing your consumption or eliminating it altogether.
Although I've considered eliminating caffeine from my diet, I feel
the same way as one mom I interviewed who said, "Caffeine is my
only vice. Don't mess with it!" If it's more than a mild or moderate
vice for you and you know you need to do something about it, follow
these guidelines by Mike Breus, Ph.D, designed to help you "fade out"
your caffeine addiction:

1. Consume caffeine regularly for a week while keeping a
   precise log of the times and amounts you drink or eat
   (include items such as chocolate, tea, soda, and caffeinated headache pills).

2. At the end of the week, start reducing your caffeine
   intake little by little by avoiding the equivalent of one-
   half cup of regular coffee (40 milligrams of caffeine)
   a day. Remember to have reduced-caffeine or zero-
   caffeine substitutes on hand for those times of day

you're accustomed to drinking a caffeinated beverage. (Such as decaf hot chocolate or herbal tea.)
Note: if possible, avoid decaf coffee too much, since it's highly acidic and could increase levels of fat in the blood.

3. If you can tolerate it, start replacing some of those additional cups of coffee (beyond the half-cup reduction per day) with a lower-caffeine drink, such as tea. Black tea has half the caffeine of coffee or carbonated caffeinated drinks like Coke or Pepsi—approximately 40 to 60 milligrams of caffeine per cup. It's also easier on the digestive system and is rich in antioxidants, which can help prevent cancer and heart disease.[6]

Many of the items mentioned in this chapter are free and effective. Focusing on exposure to sunlight, sleep, sex, and exercise are powerful ways to ensure that serotonin production is adequate, which helps stabilize mood. When combined with limiting caffeine, alcohol, and stress, we *can* control some aspects of the severity of PMS.

It's a good news/bad news situation. The good news is that we can take control and make positive changes. The bad news is that PMS may have compromised our ability to do so, thereby trying to hold us hostage to our hormones. Again, embrace the idea of making easy lifestyle changes first, followed by the more difficult ones. In my case, I focused first on getting to bed earlier and spending more time outdoors when the sun shines. Though small, these changes are making a noticeable difference for me. And the more positive difference I see, the more motivated I am to continue to impact my PMS symptoms.

Supplements

In addition to lifestyle changes, you may also consider adding a supplement to your diet. When I began my PMS research, I believed this might be the easiest way to make a quick change. Now I'm not so sure.

Much of the available literature on supplements conflicts. That makes it difficult to know which, if any, should be considered. The U.S. Food and Drug Administration doesn't strictly regulate herbs and supplements. Consequently, there is no guarantee of strength, purity, or safety of these products. Despite this, there are some herbal supplements that have been shown to reduce the severity of PMS symptoms. I've chosen to focus on two of these because I found ample evidence of their efficacy, and the physicians I interviewed were comfortable recommending them.

Black Cohosh has long been used for a variety of menstrual disorders. The plant is beautiful and drooping with white flower clusters and is native to the United States. The medicinal part is the root. Dr. Ron Eaker recommends a brand called Remifemin, which is an over-the-counter product. He notes that "the safety of black cohosh is exceptional and has been studied and documented in over sixty years of use in Germany."[7]

Though noted more for use in menopausal women (to help with hot flashes, vaginal dryness, and mood changes), it's also a natural way to address depression and anxiety in women with PMS. Notes Dr. Eaker, "I have seen moderate success with its use in women who tend to have a preponderance of emotional symptoms with PMS... It is felt that because black cohosh is a phytoestrogen, it balances the estrogen/progesterone ratio and thus improves the emotional impact of the luteal phase shift."[8]

WebMd notes, "One study has shown that black cohosh relieves PMS symptoms of anxiety, tension, and depression."[9] Black cohosh is generally dosed at one tablet twice a day (20 mg per tablet) during the luteal, or week before menstruation, phase. If improvement doesn't occur in the first month, it's allowable to increase the dosage to two tablets twice a day (up to 80 mg).

Though two physicians I spoke with recommend black cohosh to patients, author Pamela Smith, RD, offers this caution:

> Black cohosh may elevate liver enzymes, suggesting it may adversely affect the liver, along with stomach upsets,

headaches, dizziness, and weight gain. It's unknown whether black cohosh has any effect, positive or negative, on breast cancer risk. And it is also not clear whether women taking birth control pills or hormone replacement therapy can safely take black cohosh.[10]

Despite her warning, she also noted that a study published in the March 28, 2002 *Journal of Women's Health and Gender-Based Medicine* found that Remifemin reduced symptoms in 70 percent of women.

St. John's wort is a plant with yellow flowers that is often used as an herbal remedy for depression. According to the Mayo Clinic website, "Numerous studies report St. John's wort to be more effective than placebo and equally effective as tricyclic antidepressant drugs in the short-term treatment of mild-to-moderate major depression (1 to 3 months)." But the website also noted, "Recently, controversy has been raised by two high-quality trials of St. John's wort for major depression that did not show any benefits. However, due to problems with the designs of these studies, they cannot be considered definitive. Overall, the scientific evidence supports the effectiveness of St. John's wort in mild-to-moderate major depression."[11] One of these studies was sponsored by the National Center for Complementary Medicine at the National Institutes of Health, which is conducting further studies regarding the effectiveness of St. John's wort in treating depression.

Overall, the Mayo Clinic website gave St. John's wort a grade of "C" for PMS use (which indicates "unclear scientific evidence for this use"), noting that "one small study suggests that St. John's wort may be effective in reducing symptoms of premenstrual syndrome (PMS). Further studies are needed before a recommendation can be made."[12]

If you decide to try St. John's wort, note that it may take two to four weeks before you notice improvement. More important, it can cause many serious interactions with prescription drugs (including birth control pills and antidepressants), herbs, and supplements. Consult your healthcare professional and pharmacist before starting therapy, and be sure to include it on your health history any time you seek medical care.

Making Sense of What We've Learned

There's a lot to consider when it comes to unlocking the mystery of serotonin. Thankfully, much of what promotes its production is free, and, if we plan accordingly, easy to work into our schedules. Selecting a supplement is trickier. As I write this, I have six reference books on my desk, and my Internet browser is open to WebMD, Family Doctor, and the Mayo Clinic site. It's easy to find conflicting evidence and difficult to find consensus when it comes to herbal supplements. After sorting my way through the available material, I advocate a four-tiered approach to PMS management:

> *First Tier:* Focus on good nutrition, stress reduction, and exercise since research confirms consensus that these are the three most effective ways to help manage PMS.

> *Second Tier:* Promote serotonin production through sleep, sunlight, and sex.

> *Third Tier:* Measure and reduce or eliminate caffeine and alcohol intake.

> *Fourth Tier:* If none of these provide adequate relief, discuss options such as antidepressants, birth control pills, black cohosh, and St. John's wort with your physician. Your comfort level and knowledge about your situation will help determine if you prefer a prescription medication or an over-the-counter option. Whatever you try, remember that it can take weeks for noticeable improvement to occur. Furthermore, it will take patience and adjustment to find the right dosage and/or combination to address your particular symptoms.

PMS and Faith

Callie looked at the plastic bottle of purple pills on her counter. She'd filled the prescription after leaving the doctor's office. Dr. Ray told Callie that many of her patients experienced noticeable relief with this regimen. In fact, once their worst symptoms were addressed, many found the energy and ability they needed to make lasting changes to their lifestyle, resulting in further relief.

On the way home from the office, Callie recognized the "chicken or egg" dilemma. Should she take the pills in hopes of stabilizing and then work on further changing her exercise and dietary habits, or should she hold off on the medicine while waiting to see what kind of relief she would receive from the small changes she'd made so far?

Callie's quandary was complicated by her Christian faith. She believed in a personal, loving God who responded individually to prayers and requests for help. Many nights, lying awake in bed after a bad PMS day, she asked God to enlighten her and show her how to stop the monthly insanity that was compromising her ability to be the mom and wife she wanted to be. Though many of the quick prayers she uttered in the heat of the moment over the years had calmed her down and prevented further damage, she had yet to find a single solution that would put the problem behind her once and for all.

As she thought about whether or not she wanted to try the antidepressant, Callie pondered her desire to secure a "once and for all" solution. Maybe this was the problem. Since PMS was a complex challenge, maybe the solution had to be multilayered. Everything Callie was learning was pointing to no simple solutions.

But where was God in the midst of her pain? As a "good" Christian, shouldn't she be able to control her emotions more effectively without the help of medication? She knew many Christians, including her parents, who believed that prayer and gumption should be enough to handle life's challenges.

Callie remembered something she'd heard in the movie *Evan Almighty*. God, played by Morgan Freeman, offers this idea to the main character's wife, who's struggling with her husband's decision to build an ark:

> Let me ask you something. If someone prays for patience, do you think God gives them patience? Or does He give them the opportunity to be patient? If they pray for courage does God give them courage or does He give them opportunities to be courageous? If someone prays for family to be closer, do you think God zaps them with warm fuzzy feelings, or does He give them opportunities to love each other?[1]

The words made Callie wonder if, and how, PMS might develop her spiritually. Was it possible she might be maturing as a result of her struggle? It seemed like a crazy thought, but it made her feel better to think that her experience with premenstrual syndrome could result in personal growth for her rather than serving no purpose other than to make her and her family miserable each month.

Though Callie wanted God to totally eliminate her monthly symptoms, she realized that probably wasn't realistic. Perhaps she should focus instead on the fact that God provided tools she could use to help manage her symptoms. She stared again at the pills. Were these one of those tools?

Callie had broached the subject with her husband, Steve, the night before in anticipation of her appointment with Dr. Ray. If Steve had any reservations, she wanted to know. When she asked what he thought, he simply said, "Whatever you decide, Callie, is fine with me. I trust your judgment." She considered it a nonanswer and was aggravated that he hadn't been more helpful. When she pressed him further, he said, "I believe God sometimes works through medicine, if that's what you're asking." Then he changed the subject.

Since Steve hadn't been much help, Callie decided she needed a woman's point of view and elected to call her sister for advice. Esther was six years older and, though the two women hadn't lived in the same house for years, they remained close.

As Callie dialed the phone, she wondered if her sibling had difficulty with PMS. She didn't remember her mom suffering from it, but recalled that sometimes her mom would cry for no apparent reason. It happened infrequently so Callie was never concerned. Now she wondered if there was a connection. She thought about her poor father, the sole male surviving among three hormonal females. She wondered what kind of tales he could tell about that!

Esther picked up on the second ring. "Hello!"

Callie felt better just hearing her voice. "Hi, Ess. It's Callie." As a child, Callie couldn't pronounce her sister's name. She had consequently shortened it, and the nickname stuck.

"Hi! That's weird. I was just thinking about you!"

"What were you thinking? About how charming, witty, funny, and delightful I am?" Callie responded playfully.

"No. Actually, I was wondering what you'd like for your birthday since I know it's coming up."

"How about a girls' day out?" suggested Callie. Though the sisters lived several hours away from one another, they occasionally managed to meet at a spot between them for some sister time.

"Ooohhh. I like that idea!" bubbled Esther. "It's a gift to me too when we do that. I'll check with Frank to see what his schedule looks like."

"Great!" replied Callie. "I should call you more often!"

"I'm sure you weren't calling about your birthday present," noted Esther. "What's up?"

Callie was quiet for a moment and then took a deep breath. "I need some advice, Ess. I've been suffering from PMS for some time now, but it's getting worse. I don't even recognize myself sometimes. I'm angry. I'm sad. I'm depressed. I hate being a wife and mom. Those days are really, really dark. So dark, in fact, that I'm afraid to be around the kids for fear of doing or saying something I'll regret.

"I went to my doctor yesterday, and she gave me a prescription for anti-depressants. I'm just not sure I should take them," Callie finished.

"Why not?" asked Esther.

"Well, even though I'm an adult, I know mom and dad don't approve of them. And honestly, I'm not sure what I think about them. I should be able to conquer this PMS problem on my own. If I just try harder or pray more, I should be able to get it together. But then another month goes by with a nasty rant, and I get frustrated that it's still not under control and my family suffers because of it. They deserve better than that."

Esther was silent for a moment. "Cal, would it make a difference to you if you knew I've been on an antidepressant for years?"

Callie was stunned. Could it be? Her older sister on Prozac? Never in a million years did she think it was possible.

"You have?" asked Callie.

"Yes."

"Why?"

"For depression."

"Does it help?"

"Absolutely," replied Esther.

The two women were silent for a moment. Callie was the first to speak. "Yes, Esther, it helps immensely knowing you're on an antidepressant because I felt so alone in making this decision. I don't want to be dependent on medicine; I want to be in control of my life. But I don't know what to do about my severe mood swings."

"That's exactly where I found myself too," noted Esther. "I was in college. A darkness settled over me that I couldn't shake. There were days I didn't even get out of bed. When I did, I was listless and apathetic. Sometimes I just sat by the window in my dorm room and stared out at the world, not feeling like I was part of it in any significant way. My roommate was concerned and urged me to go to the health clinic."

"And?" prompted Callie.

"I went, thankfully. There was a wonderful young doctor there named Dr. Gordon. She took my concerns seriously and spent a lot of time asking questions and listening to me. She suggested an antidepressant. I was mortified. Like you, I didn't want to be 'dependent,' and I knew mom and dad would never approve. I thanked her but told her I wasn't interested."

"What did she say?" asked Callie.

"She took her card and wrote down the number of the direct line to her office on the back," recalled Esther. "She said if I changed my mind to give her a call. She wouldn't require another office visit; she'd call the prescription in for me if it was within the next two months. She said she understood my hesitation but hoped I'd keep my options open. I took the card and hid it in my pillowcase."

"Then what?" pressed Callie.

"I caught a ride home for the weekend. I tried to talk to mom and dad about how I was doing. Mom seemed concerned, but dad just brushed it off as stress from school. Even when I told him I was having trouble getting out of bed and getting through each day, he didn't seem concerned. Because I was afraid to tell him I was thinking about taking an antidepressant, I told him my roommate was. I couldn't afford the medication on my own so I needed his approval and help. He told me my roommate should 'pull herself up by her bootstraps.' You know, that old talk we've heard before. Needless to say, I put the thought of antidepressants out of my mind and headed back to school, determined to start fresh."

"And?"

"I lasted about a week. Then I was back to the depressed and apathetic state that made it almost impossible for me to function. One Friday night, when my roommate was on a date, I called the number on the back of the card Dr. Gordon gave me. Unbelievably, she was on call and answered her phone. I took that as a positive sign. She remembered me. She called in the prescription, and I picked it up the next morning. I started taking the pills that day, and I've never looked back."

"How come you've never told me this?"

"At first I was afraid you'd tell mom and dad. Plus I was embarrassed that I needed this kind of help. Eventually it just became part of my routine, and I didn't really think about it." Esther paused. "Callie, if I'd known you were struggling, I would have shared this with you sooner."

"Well, I'm glad you're sharing it now. And not just because it helps me with my own decision. I'm your sister, and I love you. I'm so sorry you went through all that alone."

"I really wasn't alone, Callie. God was with me every step of the way. I believe He led me, through my roommate, to Dr. Gordon. And I don't believe it was a coincidence that she was on call the night I decided to take action. Then, soon after I started taking the medicine, another friend told me she was on them too. I learned that silence is the enemy of healing."

"What did you just say?" Callie asked, stunned.

"Silence is the enemy of healing. When I finally admitted I had a problem, I got help. And I got better. Keeping it to myself didn't do anything. Seeking help did."

"What you said…that silence is the enemy of healing…it's the same thing my friend Amber told me when I talked to her!"

"Really? I thought I made that up!" Esther replied.

"Nope. Amber said it to me too! Great minds think alike, I guess."

"Then it must be true. Either that or you're just a slow learner, and you needed to hear it twice!" Esther laughed.

"So you think it's okay for me to try these pills." It was more of a statement than a question.

"I can't answer that for you, Callie. But I can tell you that my life changed dramatically after I'd been taking the medicine for a couple of weeks. I was able to get caught up in my classes and find the energy to do what I hadn't done for a long time. As I started to feel better, I was able to help myself more. Eventually my doctor decreased the dosage, but I still take the medicine daily."

"I guess I'll give them a try. I wonder what mom and dad would think if they knew both their daughters were taking pills?"

"Oh, I'm glad you said that. Here's the really interesting part of my story. Remember a couple of years ago when dad had prostate surgery and he just wasn't himself afterward? And we were worried about him? We figured time helped him recover from the surgery. Well, he pulled me aside that Thanksgiving and apologized for being so insensitive when I was in college. He regretted not taking me more seriously. Then he told me that after his surgery he'd wrestled with depression himself. His doctor gave him a prescription for antidepressants, which helped him get over the hump. He took them for about eight months and then tapered off until he stopped taking them altogether. I confessed that I was on them too. He asked what color mine were and confided his were blue and yellow. We had a good laugh over that. We've never spoken about it again, but I thought it was big of him to apologize and brave of him to tell me he was using them himself, especially after he and mom disapproved of them for so many years."

Tears rolled down Callie's cheeks. She didn't feel so alone anymore. Everyone wrestles with something—even her strong father. She wished she'd known so she could have visited or called more during that time and been a more active part of his recovery. "Ess, any more surprises for me?"

"No, I think I'll save the rest of our family secrets for when we get together for your birthday," Esther teased. "I'm glad you called today."

"I am too! I love you."

"Love you too! I'll talk to Frank about our 'date' and will call back when I have some possible days nailed down. Talk to you then!" With that Esther hung up the phone.

As Callie placed the phone back in its cradle, she shook her head. *It's funny how God works. I was afraid of what Mom and Dad would think, yet my parents have unknowingly given me permission to try the medicine. Amazing!*

H as your struggle with PMS been helped or hindered by your faith? This question is worth exploring. Faith should free you, not hinder or hold you back. Faith often helps us determine what is acceptable and what's not. Other people do too. When Jan Dravecky's husband, a pitcher for the San Francisco Giants, faced the amputation of his pitching arm due to a cancerous tumor, Jan was deeply affected. She began a battle of her own with panic attacks, anxiety, and depression. Note what she writes about the experience: "I had never known anyone who had experienced something like this, and as a committed Christian, I didn't understand how this could be happening to me. Guilt engulfed me. I felt alone, confused, and scared. I needed a lifeline. I needed to be shown the way up and out."[2]

Jan also experienced the phenomenon that "silence is the enemy of healing" since she didn't know anyone who felt the way she did. Because others weren't talking about their experiences, Jan assumed hers was unique. Thankfully, much has changed since her experience, and she is one of many Christians who are speaking up and sharing their stories and struggles for the benefit of others with similar journeys.

As Jan discovered, God meets us in the midst of our challenges. He provides tangible help and sources of hope in the form of the Holy Spirit, His Word, and prayer. Let's take a look at each of these tools.

The Holy Spirit

Shortly before His death, Jesus promised His disciples that He would send the Holy Spirit to them. He said, "I will ask the Father, and he will give you another Counselor to be with you forever—the Spirit of truth. The world cannot accept him, because it neither sees him nor knows him. But you know him, for he lives with you and will be in you" (John 14:16-17).

I like the idea of the Holy Spirit as Counselor, as One who provides guidance. I have peace knowing He lives with me and in me. That's also the Holy Spirit's purpose for you—to dwell in you and provide help in navigating life. I can't think of a better copilot! And yet sometimes I sell God short, thinking He's not interested in the minutiae of my daily life or the details of my struggles. After all, with billions of people on earth, how could He possibly be interested? But Jesus addressed this:

> So I say to you: Ask and it will be given to you; seek and you will find; knock and the door will be opened to you. For everyone who asks receives; he who seeks finds; and to him who knocks, the door will be opened.
>
> Which of you fathers, if your son asks for a fish, will give him a snake instead? Or if he asks for an egg, will give him a scorpion? If you then, though you are evil, know how to give good gifts to your children, how much more will your Father in heaven give the Holy Spirit to those who ask him! (Luke 11:9-13).

One commentary on this passage said, "These are not blank-check promises that God will give us anything we want, but promises that requests for our spiritual welfare will be heard. The reference to the Holy Spirit in verse 13 shows this spiritual emphasis. God is especially willing to give spiritual aid to those who seek it."[3]

God is especially willing to give spiritual aid to those who seek it. If you believe this, as I do, then it makes sense that God is willing to meet us in the midst of PMS. I know it may feel strange to ask for His help for premenstrual syndrome, but He already knows we struggle with it. Instead of hiding this fact, why not invite Him into the very space that causes us pain?

Through our invitation to Him transformation begins. When we invite Jesus into our lives, our spiritual journey begins and continues. When we invite Him into our circumstances, help comes.

Jesus promises that the Father will give the Holy Spirit to those who ask. Because of that, we have the confidence of knowing the Spirit dwells in us. Yet we still try to handle things on our own rather than accessing the supernatural power that lives in us. Think about what would happen if we could…if we would…more effectively rely on the Holy Spirit in addition to the other tools God has provided: It's an exciting possibility.

Romans 8:26 tells us, "In the same way, the Spirit helps us in our weakness. We do not know what we ought to pray for, but the Spirit himself intercedes for us with groans that words cannot express." Not only does the Spirit provide guidance, but He will intercede on our behalf. When we don't know what to pray for, the Spirit does. That's powerful!

My biggest hang-up is the issue of self-reliance vs. surrender. By trying to control what happens to me premenstrually, I limit the possibility for resolution. But what if I could truly surrender the whole issue to Christ? What would happen then? Joanna Weaver, author of *Having a Mary Spirit,* writes:

> When we stop trying to manhandle our circumstances and start giving them to God, something incredible happens. God takes everything we give Him and begins to work on our behalf. Because we've chosen to believe and trust rather than doubt and fear, He makes all of it—the good and the bad—count *for* us rather than against us.[4]

I confess that my pride sometimes keeps me from giving my circumstances to God. I believe He deserves better than the muddled mess

I am in the midst of PMS. But maybe it's not my circumstances—or my response to them—that God wants. Maybe He just wants me. All of me. Author Delores Leckey suggests that "ultimately surrender is not about giving up, but about choosing life. Suffering in some form is often the context for surrender because it can move us to be really open. Where we are extremely vulnerable we encounter our greatest strength."[5]

Is this really possible? That we encounter our greatest strength when we're most vulnerable? It seems unbelievable. And yet the apostle Paul, who persecuted Christians before becoming one himself after encountering God, wrote:

> There was given me a thorn in my flesh, a messenger of Satan, to torment me. Three times I pleaded with the Lord to take it away from me. But he said to me, "My grace is sufficient for you, for my power is made perfect in weakness." Therefore I will boast all the more gladly about my weaknesses, so that Christ's power may rest on me. That is why, for Christ's sake, I delight in weaknesses, in insults, in hardships, in persecutions, in difficulties. For when I am weak, then I am strong (2 Corinthians 12:7-10).

Paul, one of God's most ardent followers, had a "thorn in his flesh"! I find that to be an odd comfort, especially since He goes on to reveal that God's power is made perfect in weakness.

Yes, it's hard to see God in PMS, or in cancer, or diabetes, or any other illness. And yet Paul's words give us hope that illness is not in vain. That in our physical weakness we may, through Christ, find a way to become spiritually strong. Perhaps that's the very reason God sends His Holy Spirit—to help us embrace the opportunity to move from weak to strong even though there may be the personal cost of total surrender.

Surrender isn't a one-time experience. We must consciously do it on a daily basis—and sometimes even minute to minute. Daily we must make the decision to follow Christ and give everything we are to Him.

Why is surrender so hard? Because we're busy. We're distracted. We're self-sufficient. More than anything, we fear that relinquishing control will result in our being out of control. What we must learn is that because of our faith, being out of our own control means being fully in God's control. As we allow the Holy Spirit's presence to infuse our lives, we will become more certain of this. The act of continual, deliberate surrender gets easier and the "tool" of tapping the Holy Spirit's power begins to feel natural and useful in our hands.

Because the Holy Spirit isn't something tangible or something we "do" (such as prayer) or something we read (such as the Bible), this element of spiritual growth is the least understood and the least sought. I believe the Holy Spirit is an untapped power source for many of us. Imagine having the "Spirit of Truth" sent by God to "live with you and in you." Incredible! Instead of acting on our own, we have a Counselor who is with us day in and day out, one who is willing to assist, to encourage, and to help us grapple with life. When combined with the other tools discussed in this chapter, we see the power we have within is not our own power, but God's power.

God's Word

The Bible tells the story of our personal, loving God who sent His Son, Jesus, to die on a cross for our sins so that we can live with God eternally. The story sounds a little crazy on paper, but our faith informs our decisions and is in every fiber of our being. Yet we often forget the nuances of the story or the reminders that God provides so that we don't lose hope or give up. Thankfully, the Bible serves as a handy resource—and another of God's tools—that we can use in the midst of the darkness of PMS, as well as in everyday life.

Though God never promises an easy journey, He does promise that He will be with us *every step* of the way. Psalm 139 is one of my favorite Bible passages, especially verses 7 through 10:

> Where can I go from your Spirit?
>> Where can I flee from your presence?
> If I go up to the heavens, you are there;
>> if I make my bed in the depths, you are there.
> If I rise on the wings of the dawn,
>> if I settle on the far side of the sea,
> even there your hand will guide me,
>> your right hand will hold me fast.

Even in the throes of PMS we are in God's presence. Furthermore, His right hand holds us fast when we are out of control. Though my PMS behavior causes me shame, it's comforting to know I'm being held by Someone who loves me and cares about me. If only I could be more mindful of that when I'm in the depths! Psalm 139 is just one of hundreds of passages and verses that offer comfort and assurance for God's children.

God speaks to us through His Word, initiating transformation in us and through us. Romans 12:2 instructs, "Do not conform any longer to the pattern of this world, but be transformed by the renewing of your mind. Then you will be able to test and approve what God's will is—his good, pleasing and perfect will." The renewing of our minds comes, in part, through reading God's story. But the Bible is also *our* story since our response to it shapes us, our faith, and our actions. What we learn through the Bible, though written long ago, is relevant today. Eugene Peterson, translator of *The Message* Bible and author of *Run with the Horses,* informs us that...

> the Bible makes it clear that every time there is a story of faith, it is completely original. God's creative genius is endless. He never, fatigued and unable to maintain the rigors of creativity, resorts to mass-producing copies. Each life is a fresh canvas on which he uses lines and colors, shades and light, textures and proportions that he has never used before.[6]

You and I are fresh creations, and God's story is being told through our stories. We can influence the narrative by reading the Bible and using what we learn in our daily lives. We must read with an inquiring mind, asking ourselves:

- What can I learn?
- What can I use today?
- What do I need to know?
- How does this affect me?
- What characteristics of this biblical person do I possess?
- What can I learn from his or her story?

As we let the words of the Bible fill our hearts and resound in our minds, we open the door to personal growth and change. We challenge the status quo and invite new knowledge into our lives. The very act of opening The Book, reading it, and studying it in-depth brings order and discipline to us. First, the discipline required to get to the point of opening the book changes us. Then the words and stories themselves change us. It's mystical and difficult to describe, mostly because the effect is personal, private, and as unique as each one of us.

If you're not familiar with the Bible, consider digging into it, learning more about God's promises and your response to them. Though I've been reading the Bible for years, I'm still surprised at how the same words speak to me in new ways each time I read them. As my situation and circumstances change, I notice things I've never noted before and receive assurances for the state I'm in, such as the fact that God says, "I have engraved you on the palms of my hands" (Isaiah 49:16) and that even the hairs on my head are numbered (Matthew 10:30). These images are comforting, especially when the darkness of PMS clouds my sight.

Prayer

Prayer puts God at the center of our lives and invites Him into our daily experiences. This is the most intimate form of communication that we as humans can participate in. Think about how incredible it is that we can approach the Creator of the Universe and converse with Him personally, intimately, and privately. What a privilege! The problem many of us face is that we're too busy and get caught up in our daily lives so we forget to pray and forget to spend time listening for God's response. My prayer life suffers because I'm busy. And sometimes I don't know how to pray. Because I feel inadequate, ashamed, or disappointed in myself, it sometimes is difficult for me to speak to my heavenly Father. But even as I consider how lacking my prayer life is, I know this to be true:

> Turning life into words to share with the Most High is not for the faint of heart. It requires confidence in our ability to approach Him and faith that He will not disappoint us. Prayer is the vehicle by which we cement our connection with Him. It's the means by which we keep our relationship flourishing. Through it, we also begin to really understand ourselves and embrace who God made us to be. An active prayer life leads to an intimate relationship with God.[7]

I want my relationship with God to flourish. I want it to be intimate. The way to ensure this happens is to speak to Him regularly, honestly, and specifically. Then, since communication is a two-way street, I must listen for His response. Listening requires stillness, but being still is something I hardly know how to do...and maybe you can relate.

My best ideas and greatest understandings come when I am at rest, especially when it comes to writing. Yet I feel most alive when I am in motion. What a conundrum! Do I sit still hoping for an idea or do I move in order to make something happen each day? The answer, I know, is both. This is also difficult. Movement combined with times of tranquility leads to balance.

Author Richard Bode learned the value of stillness when he was in a body cast for six months while recovering from surgery. He writes, "Day after day, as I lay in my enforced idleness, I thought deeply about who I was, where I came from, and what I wanted to be. What I had lost in physical motion I had gained in insight, which is movement of another kind. I learned the interior life was as rewarding as the exterior life, and that my richest moments occurred when I was absolutely still."[8]

Prayer allows us to explore the crevices of our interior life. Stillness allows us to hear God's response. Yet stillness is the antithesis of today's culture, which encourages us to do more, be more, achieve more. It is usually in the quiet times that God comes and speaks to our hearts, gently letting us know He is present and He hears us.

Sometimes the very things we need are the things we are least able to reach for. This is true with prayer. Often the very thing we need—to connect verbally with God—is thwarted by our own views, or pride, or shame, making it *seem* impossible to present ourselves before Him.

Though I've mastered the art of the "Arrow Prayer" (shooting a quick request directly to heaven while in the midst of turmoil), it's the more lengthy, in-depth ones I struggle with. I suspect it's because these deep prayers require time, focus, and a willingness to sit still before the Lord. But deep prayers are transforming prayers, and it's this type of prayer life I aspire to.

As I've researched and worked on this book, I elected to be a guinea pig and try all the methods of managing PMS that I'm writing about. I'm more conscious of my food choices. I'm making sure some form of physical activity is on my agenda every day. (Does "waking up" count as exercise? It should—on some days at least!) I'm alert to potentially stressful situations and choosing to change these circumstances or avoid them. And I start each day by acknowledging God's presence and inviting the Holy Spirit into my daily life. Although this last one is a habit I've had off and on through the years, I now realize that I don't take advantage of its full potential.

Perhaps I'm making prayer too hard. Instead of waiting for a deep, lengthy dialogue, maybe it's enough to turn my thoughts heavenward several times a day and talk to God like I talk to myself. That way God and I have a running dialogue rather than the stilted conversations we sometimes have that are as awkward as those held between friends who haven't seen each other for a long time. "Prayer is like a muscle. If you exercise it regularly, your prayer muscle will gain strength and your appreciation for God will grow immeasurably. On the other hand, if you don't use it, your prayer muscle will shrivel up and your capacity for God will shrink."[9]

The Bible teaches me, the Holy Spirit guides me, and prayer offers a new sense of peace and confidence that settles me, even in my most anxious moments. I am humbled at the idea that I can capture the ear of God...and blessed by that very same thought. I'm still growing in my prayer life, and I'm encouraged that even short moments on my knees hold such great power.

Hebrews 4:16 says, "Let us then approach the throne of grace with confidence, so that we may receive mercy and find grace to help us in our time of need." One of my deepest times of need is when I'm premenstrual. I used to be ashamed of that fact, but no longer. I have confidence that God is in the depths with me and that, with His help, I can climb out of the pit each month. And since you're reading this book, you may be able to relate. As our confidence in finding practical ways to cope grows, so will our willingness to invite God into the situations we find ourselves in, whether PMS-related or not.

Reaching for God is a life choice. A decision. Will we continue to try to tackle PMS on our own or will we surrender the problem to God for our own benefit and the good of our families?

What Is Victory?

PMS is humbling. It's hard to realize and admit we're not always in control. It's difficult to acknowledge that we are less than perfect. And it's scary to think about how our PMS affects our families. Is it possible that "conquering" PMS is less about overcoming the symptoms we face each month and more about crafting a positive and proactive response? That victory isn't about taming our physical and emotional symptoms, but instead focusing on the condition of our hearts as we live through our difficult days each month?

As I've looked at the PMS issue from a spiritual standpoint, I've begun to see it less as something to be overcome and more as something that gives me the opportunity to walk in more reliance on God. Knowing I can't control the symptoms of PMS on my own causes me to stretch out my hands and ask Him to hold them in the midst of my monthly physical and emotional pain. I confess it's a struggle for me to do this. I'd rather be self-sufficient. But when I am weak, then Jesus is strong. There's a brilliant blessing in my weakness in that it encourages me to rely on the One who is stronger than anything. Colossians 1:17 tells us, "He is before all things, and in him all things hold together."

The fact is, God holds each of us together each minute, each hour, each day. We covet His love, His involvement, His peace. PMS can remind us of this each month if we let it. We can loathe that hard time or give in to the lessons there are for us to learn in the midst of it. Yes, it's amazing that something so potentially debilitating holds blessings within it, but it reaffirms what we know about God: He loves His children! Each day He surprises us by giving us what we need when we need it, if we let Him.

15

Examining Your Legacy

Callie sat on the deck watching her girls roll snowballs in the yard. They had awakened to a fresh snowfall that morning, and Callie had barely been able to get them to eat breakfast before they were dragging their leggings from the hall closet to the back sliding doors. Abby knew the snow routine; Jessica mimicked her older sister. The three females suited up and headed into the snow before Steve even left the house for work.

Now, as Callie took a break, she studied her children. She wondered how two children, born to the same parents and living in the same house, could be so different. Abby was blonde with blue eyes. Jessica was brunette with large brown eyes. Abby preferred keeping to herself and had a hard time in new situations. Jessica never met a stranger and even with her limited vocabulary, was able to strike up a conversation with anyone, anywhere. In fact, Steve and Callie often worried that Jessica would grab the hand of a stranger and be gone before they knew it.

Callie thought of her sister and how different they were. As she looked at her girls, she wondered what kind of women they would grow up to be. Having children was an awesome job. Callie knew she was influencing them without even realizing it. The other day Abby turned to her and said, "Let's make a wise choice, Mom." It was a phrase Callie used often with the girls without even thinking about it. Now Abby was parroting it back. It made Callie mindful of the words she used. She realized her actions were subject to the same mimicking and wondered about that too. Would Abby and Jessica remember the yelling, the crying, and the tirades when she struggled with PMS? Or would her influence on the girls be more positive now that she was taking steps to limit the negatives of PMS?

She realized that in addition to crafting her own healthy PMS response, someday she'd help the girls do the same. She wished her own mother had been more open about discussing difficult subjects and resolved to be the kind of mom whose children could ask her anything.

A snowball hit Callie, knocking her out of her reverie. "Who threw that?" she demanded as she rose off the deck in one swift movement, roaring like a monster. "I'm gonna get you both!" She yelled laughingly and heard the squeals of delight from the kids. And Callie was off, running through the snow.

A s one of our children's primary influences, we are role models for them 24 hours a day, 7 days a week—including our PMS times. Ouch.

My deepest mothering grief comes from the fact that my kids have seen me at my worst time and time again, on a fairly predictable schedule. I prefer not to think about what they've learned in those ugly times. I'd rather assume they learn more by watching me in my strong, rational moments than they do in my weak, out-of-control flashes. After all, I have more of the former, so that should make a difference, right? Can you relate?

As we consider the influence we're having when we're under the influence of PMS, like it or not, we are laying a foundation for our children. Their response to life often mirrors ours. So let's begin by being more honest with our kids when we fall short. We can say:

- "I handled that poorly and I'm sorry."
- "I didn't have to yell at you, did I? May I have a do-over?"
- "I could have approached that differently. Instead of flying off the handle, I wish I had _____."
- "Boy, mommy sure is grumpy today, isn't she?"

When I own up to what's really happening, my kids seem to be relieved. And they are forgiving when I apologize and responsive when I suggest a do-over or another way to handle a situation. Hopefully your children will respond the same way. By verbalizing our regrets and acknowledging that we could have done things differently, we're teaching them how to work through things when they too behave poorly or do something less than graciously. This is especially crucial when our children are nearing or are in their teens. They need positive modeling for the mixed emotions they will feel during those momentous growing years.

Sharing What's Happening with Your Children

When should we talk to our children about PMS? It doesn't make sense to do so when they are young since their ability to understand is limited. However, as they reach the tween and teen stages, it will be prudent to share some of what's happening to us.

For younger kids it may be hard to talk about "premenstrual syndrome" without explaining menstruation, but when necessary we can refer to PMS as a hormone imbalance. This worked for my children. However we choose to approach the PMS subject, we need to offer it as an *explanation* for our behavior rather than an *excuse*. Providing some specific actions our children can take to respond to us when they know we're having a tough time might help too. These include allowing us some alone time, offering to help set the table and/or clear the dinner dishes, and remaining quiet in the car.

How we handle our PMS will influence how our daughter(s) will one day handle theirs. Evidence suggests that PMS runs in families. Whatever you ask your kids to do for you during your PMS times, such as giving you some personal space, you should be willing to do for your girls. If you need time alone during PMS, allow them the same. If you're sensitive to noise or extra stimulation during your most difficult phase, your daughter may be too. Once you've identified your own needs when you're premenstrual, you'll be more able to help her identify and deal with her needs—some of which she may not be aware of. You'll be a valuable ally in helping her in this regard!

Perhaps the toughest aspect of PMS management is finding balance. PMS is real and deserves attention. However, it shouldn't become an excuse. Though we may need to limit our activities and stress levels during certain phases, society rarely lets us drop out altogether (nor would we probably want to much of the time). Our daughters need to learn the delicate dance of destressing and pulling back, yet remaining as engaged as possible during PMS. Though we may still be mastering this skill ourselves, we can teach it to our daughters through our words and actions.

All children need to hear phrases such as "There's no need to overdo it," "We don't have to do everything today," and "Let's make sure we're not rushed and have enough time to do everything well."

Practical Approaches

The knowledge you've gained about yourself will be helpful as you help your daughter cope with her PMS. The more open and factual you are about the syndrome, the less mystery it will hold for your child. As you work through your own issues, you can help your daughter identify and work through hers. The following tips should be helpful.

Name it. When PMS comes calling for anyone in your immediate family, name it. Teach your girl to identify what's happening. The sooner she makes the connection between her menstrual cycle and her emotions and behavior, the quicker she will be able to respond proactively. Be sensitive about how personal this subject might be for your daughter. Your family dynamics will determine if you share privately or with the entire household. The purpose of identifying PMS is not to provide an excuse for poor behavior or to give one family member a reason to taunt or tease another. Instead you're alerting members of the family team that a little extra kindness and tender loving care is in order for a few days. Modeling care, concern, and compassion within the family makes it more likely that your children will be able to respond to those outside the family similarly.

Acknowledge it. Younger women report a higher degree of physical complaints with PMS. If your daughter complains of menstrual cramps, headaches, backaches, nausea, and so forth, take her seriously. Some girls experience even more severe symptoms such as dizziness and vomiting, which can be debilitating. Be alert to the possibility that your daughter may need to seek medical attention if her symptoms are severe or interfere regularly with daily activities. Don't baby her, but be sympathetic as she responds to the physical symptoms of her menstrual cycle.

Dana, a mom of twins, shared that occasionally when one of her girls is experiencing severe cramps, she provides ibuprofen and allows her daughter to stay home from school until the mild pain reliever kicks in. Acknowledging symptoms and expressing sympathy are valuable ways to develop your mother/daughter relationship and let your child know she can count on you for help.

Chart it. Since we've seen the value of charting, it's wise to help your daughter chart her cycle as well. Remember: That which is predictable is preventable. When you know your daughter is struggling premenstrually, it's easier to handle her with patience and extra love. You can also quietly warn your hubby to handle her with kid gloves. Plus, you'll want to help her heed much of the same advice that helps you: more physical activity, no big decisions, no tough tasks, and extra sleep during this time.

Charting your daughter's cycle will also alert you if your cycles become synchronized, which often happens. Two (or more) premenstrual women in a household can be explosive. Knowing the two of you might be volatile at the same time is valuable information—and will require a high level of intention to keep things peaceful. It also makes it easier to prepare, plan, and schedule family activities accordingly.

If your daughter is young, she may not need to complete a detailed chart. Help her to do enough to be able to anticipate when her next period is coming for practical reasons, such as being prepared with necessary supplies. If you notice her symptoms worsening or she expresses concern or confusion about runaway emotions, show her how to track her symptoms in a more detailed manner, identify her patterns, and respond proactively.

Feed her wisely. Depending on your daughter's age, it's likely you have a strong influence over the food she eats (especially if you are the main cook in your household). Everything we've learned about wise food choices applies to your daughter. Provide plenty of fresh fruits and vegetables and encourage their consumption. (You might even go so far as cutting up fruits or vegetables for her since the effort of having to peel an orange or slice an apple makes it tempting for teens to grab crackers or chips.) Plan meals that include lean proteins, complex carbohydrates, and fiber. If she must satisfy a carbohydrate or sweets craving, encourage her to consume a little instead of a lot. Teach her to eat five smaller meals and to eat every three to four hours when possible to stabilize her blood sugar. Not only is this good for PMS, but you'll be developing healthy eating habits for her overall.

Invite her to be physically active with you. Ask her…and encourage her…to walk around the block or join you at the gym. Kids love one-on-one time with parents, and this is the perfect time for you to suggest an activity together. Not only will it possibly reduce her symptoms, but you'll be building your relationship as well.

Boys and PMS

Though girls may need the most attention when it comes to sharing PMS lessons, it's important for boys (especially those who don't grow up with sisters) to learn about premenstrual syndrome as well. After all, there's a good chance that some of their female buddies will experience it in high school, college, and beyond. Some women they date will likely have it. Coworkers may suffer from it. And it's possible they may marry a woman who struggles with PMS. As the men quoted in chapter 10 reveal, being around a woman who's friendly and open one minute and grumpy and downright rude the next, even if it is attributable to PMS, can be confusing. Helping boys understand why PMS happens and how to handle it with some sensitivity gives them a valuable foundation for interpersonal relationships that will serve them well throughout their lives.

PMS Is a Family Issue

Some people say that PMS is a women's issue, but it's not. It affects the people around her, including her husband (if she's married), and her children. It affects all relationships. It influences how we model coping skills for our children. It can interfere with care-giving responsibilities. Yes, PMS is a family issue. How we handle PMS, *whether* we deal with it or ignore it, has an impact on family dynamics. Keep that in mind as you craft a healthy response to what can be a debilitating condition.

Carefully consider how your behavior is affecting your children and how much you should reveal about your battle (in an age-appropriate way, of course). Talk with your husband about this as well. In fact, he and the kids may already have a code for "when it's that time of the month." If so, you should know.

Being open and honest about PMS is the best way to live. This makes it less of a mystery, decreases the potential for shame, and presents it as what it is: a medical condition that impacts the entire family. Though there's no need to spotlight it every month, there's no need to hide it either. A straightforward approach, presented when children are old enough to understand, makes the most sense. PMS offers a valuable opportunity to teach your children how healthy families address difficult issues: honestly and with compassion. Though we'd prefer not to have PMS, we're choosing to embrace the reality of our situation and make the best of it.

16

Loving Yourself While Living with PMS

It was a quiet, wintry morning. Abby and Jessica sat transfixed before a *My Little Pony* video in the family room, giving Callie some quiet time. Though she was within earshot of the girls, she still had the space she needed to get her journal and capture her thoughts. Instead of the desperate entries she'd written much earlier, today she planned to note the progress she was making.

Callie took a sip of her spiced orange cranberry tea and opened her notebook to the next blank page. She jotted the date at the top of the page, then wrote:

> So much has happened over the past several months. Perhaps most important is that I was finally honest with myself about my struggle with PMS. I could never imagine the changes in the last six months! I'm eating better, sleeping better, mothering better, and my relationship with Steve is better. Can PMS lead to good things? In my case, it has.
>
> I still struggle with it. But instead of losing my patience with the kids, I'm removing myself from hard situations more and more. I no longer try to make decisions when I'm tense and moody. I go to bed earlier, take more walks, and retreat to a hot bath when I need to. It's crazy that such little things have made such a big difference, but they have. I wish I'd made them sooner. The shift in my attitude has made a difference too. In addition to loving and supporting my family, I've decided that I need love and support too. That old saying "When Momma's not happy, ain't nobody happy" is true. I'm the heartbeat of this family. When I'm at peace, my family is at peace. When I'm tense, everyone else is too. I'm not sure

they realize this, but I've noticed it, especially with Steve. He gets irritable when I am, and then his irritation makes me even more grumpy.

Though I still struggle, much has changed for the better. I kicked my Mountain Dew habit. I let myself have one a week for a treat, but I'm not dependent on the caffeine like I used to be. Steve has been great about watching the kids while I exercise at night. He even got me a membership at the local fitness club. The girls go to the nursery while I work out, and I try to make it two mornings a week. I've lost eight pounds as a result, and I'm feeling so much better!

Steve has been great! Though I don't think he'll ever truly understand the morass I fall into each month, he's going out of his way to be supportive and helpful when I'm PMSing. He's started a "Daddy's Night Out" with the girls. He takes them out for a special treat when I have PMS. He comes to the door, rings the bell, and asks if Jessica and Abby are ready for their date. The girls love it! I do too. I usually veg out or read a book while they're gone, which I've hardly been able to do since the girls were born.

I didn't realize how stale and routine our marriage had become until I had what I call "My PMS Crisis." Figuring out how to respond to it made me look at every area of my life and admit what I was doing well and where I was falling short. I'm more focused now. I feel some of our earlier love coming back. I don't say yes to as many outside requests because this time with the girls will pass quickly, and they will only be this age once. I should have done this after having each of the girls—deciding what needed to change. But I didn't. PMS forced me to though. In a strange way, that was a blessing.

Another blessing is that my neighbor Amber and I are now good friends. We no longer talk just about PMS, except for an occasional joke, so our friendship is based on more than that. I love her sense of humor, and she's a fount of wisdom. The girls and I have been with her twice to see her mom. I was uncertain about taking the girls, but her mom loves them! We've started walking together on weekends, and we talk by phone at least once a week. She's been a godsend.

One other thing worth noting: My relationship with me and with

God has changed. I don't feel like I have to be in total control anymore (just 99.9%! Ha!). I felt so hopeless when all this PMS started. Yet now I have hope. It's like the Bible says in Philippians 4:7—the peace of God surpasses all understanding. I truly don't understand it, but I like it.

I don't always have it, but I know I can. Sometimes it may be slight in the midst of PMS, but it's strong the rest of the month, which reminds me that my mental state during PMS is temporary, and I don't have to give in to it. I only have to get through it. One minute, one hour, one day at a time.

Before she finished, Callie's quiet time was interrupted by Abby's voice screaming, "Moooooom! The video is over!" Callie closed the journal and put down her pen. *Back to work,* she thought. *A mother's job truly never ends.*

Callie has reached an important milestone in her personal PMS planning: She recognizes she's the heartbeat of her family. Because of that, she knows her physical and emotional health is important, and she's now willing to make it the priority it should be.

Jesus addressed the issue of self-care, as recorded in the book of Matthew. When a religious leader asked Him a question designed to trick Him, He answered with wisdom for all ages and all times:

> "Teacher, which is the greatest commandment in the Law?"
>
> Jesus replied: "Love the Lord your God with all your heart and with all your soul and with all your mind." This is the first and greatest commandment. And the second is like it: "Love your neighbor as yourself" (Matthew 22:36-39).

This verse stopped me in my tracks after I became a mother. Tired of cleaning up vomit and waiting on people hand and foot, this scripture told me I mattered. I wasn't just supposed to love everyone else, I was supposed to love them *as I love myself.*

"As yourself." Two little words—but so powerful! Have you wondered, like I have, if Jesus, having walked on earth as a man, got a sense of the struggle it can be to love ourselves? Did He wrestle with self-loathing? Or with disappointment in Himself? Or experience a sense of futility? Bible experts would probably answer no because He was both God and man. But I wonder. Why didn't He just say, "Love your neighbor?" Why did He add the words "as yourself"?

Is self-love required before we can love others? Does an understanding that we also matter make it easier to give and receive love? Jesus doesn't *ask* us to love ourselves as our neighbors—He *commands* it. It's precisely because of this command that we need to add ourselves to our list of priorities. When I first became a mom I had the false sense that I no longer mattered, that to be a good mom I had to put my family first all the time. It felt selfish to take time out for me—to make time for physical activity, to want time alone in order to regroup, and to get adequate sleep. I'm sure you can relate. But now I understand that it's impossible for us to pour ourselves out on our families if we're empty. Jesus understood this. Repeatedly we read about Him "withdrawing" to rest and pray. He didn't heal everyone before Him, and He didn't work until He dropped from exhaustion. He took care of Himself so He could care for others. Even though Jesus wasn't a mother, He is a perfect mothering model.

Moms, if there is ever a time for self-care, it's when we are premenstrual. Making ourselves a priority during this time has many benefits, not only for us but for our families. We'll be less likely to strike out. Instead of feeling hopeless and helpless, we'll nurture inner strength. We'll be more likely to remain steady rather than exhibiting the roller coaster emotions that confuse our family members. Our determination will translate to self-control that we haven't always exercised in the past. And on those occasions when we lose the PMS battle, we'll understand that a misstep today doesn't have to lead to another one tomorrow.

A healthy approach to life helps mitigate PMS. We must take care of ourselves to take care of our families in the best way possible. When we take care of ourselves through good nutrition, exercise, and stress reduction, we're also indirectly providing a healthy, patient, even-tempered mom for our children. What's good for you is good for them! When you get what you need, they'll get what they need. This is a marvel of God's perfect design.

Positive, Meaningful, Significant

Yesterday, while taking a walk on a snowy day, I contemplated the awesome truth that we are children of God and He cares about us. We matter, our spouses matter, and our children matter. Consequently, our response to the PMS challenge also matters since it's part of our unique walk on earth. PMS can overwhelm us, or frustrate us, or be a source of growth and new understanding about ourselves and who we're called to be.

The work of our hands influences so many people inside and outside our family circle. Let's be a positive force! Take a look at what Nicole Johnson writes about this phenomenon:

> Some days I am only a pair of hands, nothing more: Can you fix this? Can you tie this? Can you open this?
>
> Some days I'm not a pair of hands; I'm not even a human being. I'm a clock to ask, "What time is it?" I'm a satellite guide to answer, "What number is the Disney Channel?" I'm a car to order, "Right around 5:30, please."
>
> I was certain that these were the hands that once held books and the eyes that studied history and the mind that graduated summa cum laude—but now they had disappeared into the peanut butter, never to be seen again.
>
> She's going...she's going...she's gone!

One night, a group of us were having dinner, celebrating the return of a friend from England. Janice had just gotten back from a fabulous trip, and she was going on and on about the hotel she stayed in. I was sitting there, looking around at the others all put together so well. It was hard not to compare and feel sorry for myself as I looked down at my out-of-style dress; it was the only thing I could find that was clean. My unwashed hair was pulled up in a banana clip, and I was afraid I could actually smell peanut butter in it. I was feeling pretty pathetic, when Janice turned to me with a beautifully wrapped package and said, "I brought you this."

It was a book on the great cathedrals of Europe. I wasn't exactly sure why she'd given it to me until I read her inscription: "To Charlotte, with admiration for the greatness of what you are building when no one sees."[1]

My friend, you and I are building great cathedrals in our children! Who knows whose lives they will touch or what they will one day accomplish? Sure, we'd rather be freed completely from PMS while building up our children. Since that's unlikely, we have the freedom to determine our responses. Will we be defeated before we begin? Or will we step up to the plate and do our very best?

It is my hope that after reading this book you'll have the confidence and ability to continue to build great things in your family *every* day. The greatest thing about the future is that you have the power to influence it. I pray that influence is *P*ositive, *M*eaningful, and *S*ignificant—your very own special *PMS*. Change begins in the moment of decision, and there's power in deciding that tomorrow will be different than today. Embrace and enjoy your journey.

Notes

Chapter 1—There's Yellow Caution Tape in the Kitchen Again

1. http://www.webmd.com/hw/womens_conditions/hw139470.asp?printing=true, September 1, 2006.

2. Susan Lark, M.D., *Premenstrual Syndrome Self Help Book* (Berkeley, CA: Celestial Arts, 1984), 13.

3. Michelle Harrison, M.D., *Self-Help for Premenstrual Syndrome* (New York: Random House, 1982), 3-4.

Chapter 2—What If It's Not PMS, and This Is Just My Personality?

1. Archibald Hart and Catherine Hart Weber, *Unveiling Depression in Women* (Grand Rapids, MI: Revell, 2001), 60.

2. Susan Lark, *Premenstrual Syndrome,* 21-22.

Chapter 3—I'm Losing My Mind, and My Daughter Wants to Go to Target?

1. Ron Eaker, M.D., *Holy Hormones* (Bristol, TN: Selah Publishing, 2000), 98.

Chapter 4—Charting Your Course and Navigating the Whitewater

1. Ron Eaker, M.D., *Holy Hormones,* 67.

Chapter 5—PMS Basics

1. As quoted in Stephanie DeGraff Bender and Kathleen Kelleher, *PMS: Women Tell Women How to Control Premenstrual Syndrome* (Oakland, CA: New Harbinger Publications, 1996), 7.

2. Ibid.

3. Lori Futterman and John E. Jones, *PMS, Perimenopause, and You* (Lincolnwood, IL: Lowell House, 2000), 22-23.

4. DeGraff Bender and Kelleher, *PMS,* 32-33.

5. Ibid., 16.

6. Ibid., 29-30.

Chapter 6—PMS S.O.S.

1. DeGraff Bender and Kelleher, *PMS,* 69.

2. Ibid., 71.

3. Pamela Smith, RD, *When Your Hormones Go Haywire* (Grand Rapids, MI: Zondervan, 2005), 148, adapted.

4. Julie Ann Barnhill, *She's Gonna Blow! Real Help for Moms Dealing with Anger* (Eugene, OR: Harvest House Publishers, 2001), 49.

Chapter 7—All Stressed Up and Everywhere to Go

1. http://womenshealth.about.com/cs/stress/a/stressbusters.htm, November 6, 2007.

2. Mary M. Byers, *How to Say No...and Live to Tell About It* (Eugene, OR: Harvest House Publishers, 2006), 86.

3. http://www.sleepfoundation.org/site/apps/nl/content2.asp?c=huIXKjM0IxF&b=2434067&ct =3618771, November 6, 2007.

4. Mary M. Byers, *The Mother Load: How to Meet Your Own Needs While Caring for Your Family* (Eugene, OR: Harvest House Publishers, 2005), 211.

5. http://www.crescentlife.com/wellness/stressors.htm, November 6, 2007.

Chapter 8—If I Am What I Eat, Does That Make Me a Donut?

1. http://womenshealth.about.com/cs/pms/a/pmssymptreatm.htm, November 8, 2007.

2. Tara W. Strine, Daniel P. Chapman, Indu B. Ahluwalia, "Menstrual-Related Problems and Psychological Distress Among Women in the United States," *Journal of Women's Health* (15409996), May 2005, vol. 14, issue 4, 316-23.

3. Lark, *Premenstrual Syndrome,* 48, 66-68.

4. Futterman and Jones, *PMS, Perimenopause, and You,* 219.

5. Ibid., 218.

6. Harley Pasternak, M.Sc., *The Five Factor Diet* (Des Moines, IA: Meredith Books, 2006), 37.

7. Ibid., 242.

8. Danna Demetre, *The Heat Is On* (Grand Rapids, MI: Revell, 2005), 100.

9. http://www.clevelandclinic.org/health/health-info/docs/2700/2731.asp?index=7250, January 2, 2008.

10. http://www.bottomlinesecrets.com/blpnet/article.html?article_id=40431, November 14, 2007.

11. http://www.lifescript.com/channels/food_nutrition/Nutrition_Tips/lose_weight_with_the_ portion_teller.asp?page=4, November 14, 2007.

12. Ibid.

13. "The Childhood Obesity Epidemic," *The Week,* November 2, 2007, 13.

Chapter 9—You've Got to Move It, Move It!

1. Smith, *When Your Hormones Go Haywire,* 243-44.

2. Futterman and Jones, *PMS, Perimenopause, and You,* 120.

Chapter 10—Let's All Just Get on the Titanic

1. DeGraff Bender and Kelleher, *PMS,* 110-12, 115.

2. Emerson Eggerichs, *Love & Respect* (Nashville, TN: Integrity Publishers, 2004), 20.

Chapter 12—To Medicate or Not

1. Eaker, *Holy Hormones,* 61.

2. http://www.radiantrecovery.com/chemistry.htm#serotonin, November 23, 2007.

3. http://www.healthyplace.com/communities/Depression/treatment/antidepressants/maoi.asp, November 21, 2007.

4. http://www.mayoclinic.com/health/antidepressants/HQ01069, November 29, 2007.

Chapter 13—The Serotonin and Supplement Mystery

1. http://www.sleepfoundation.org/atf/cf/%7BF6BF2668-A1B4-4FE8-8D1A-A5D39340 D9CB%7D/how_much_large.jpg, December 12, 2007, used by permission.

2. http://www.sleepfoundation.org/site/c.huIXKjM0IxF/b.2419223/k.38D8/Womens_Unique_Sleep_Experiences.htm, December 12, 2007.

3. http://www.sleepfoundation.org/site/c.huIXKjM0IxF/b.2419225/k.490E/Understanding_Your_Monthly_Cycle.htm, December 12, 2007.

4. http://www.sleepfoundation.org/site/c.huIXKjM0IxF/b.2421185/k.7198/Let_Sleep_Work_for_You.htm, December 12, 2007.

5. http://www.womentowomen.com/fatigueandstress/effectsofcaffeine.aspx, December 12, 2007.

6. http://www.theinsomniablog.com/the_insomnia_blog/2007/02/caffeine_fading.html, December 12, 2007.

7. Eaker, *Holy Hormones,* 179.

8. Ibid., 94.

9. http://women.webmd.com/pms/premenstrual-syndrome-pms-other-treatment, December 13, 2007.

10. Smith, *When Your Hormones Go Haywire,* 79.

11. http://www.mayoclinic.com/health/st-johns-wort/NS_patient-stjohnswort, December 13, 2007.

12. Ibid.

Chapter 14—PMS and Faith

1. *Evan Almighty,* directed by Tom Shadyac (Hollywood, CA: Universal Studios, 2007).

2. http://www.outreachofhope.org/index.cfm/PageID/362, December 1, 2007.

3. http://www.biblegateway.com/resources/commentaries/?action=getCommentaryText&cid=3&source=1&seq=i.49.10.1, December 2007, from IVP New Testament Commentary Series (InterVarsity Press), vol. 3, *Luke,* by Darrell Bock.

4. Joanna Weaver, *Having a Mary Spirit* (Colorado Springs: WaterBrook Press, 2006), 87.

5. Delores Leckey, *Seven Essentials for the Spiritual Journey* (New York: Crossroad Publishing Company, 1999), 115.

6. Eugene Peterson, *Run with the Horses: The Quest for Life at Its Best* (Downers Grove, IL: InterVarsity Press, 1983), 13.

7. Julie Clinton with Mary M. Byers, *Extraordinary Women: Secrets to Discovering the Dream God Created for You* (Eugene, OR: Harvest House Publishers, 2007), 203.

8. Richard Bode, *First You Have to Row a Little Boat* (New York: Time Warner, 1993), 79.

9. Bruce Bickel and Stan Jantz, *God Is in the Small Stuff* (Uhrichsville, OH: Promise Press, 1998), 55.

Chapter 16—Loving Yourself While Living with PMS

1. Nicole Johnson, *The Invisible Woman: When Only God Sees* (Nashville, TN: Thomas Nelson, 2005). Adapted and used from online excerpt. Used by permission of Nicole Johnson and Thomas Nelson, Inc. All rights reserved.

Join me online!

I'd love to correspond with you each month through my free online newsletter. Simply go to www.marybyers. com, click on the writing side, and share your e-mail address with me. Once a month I'll show up in your in-box with a note to encourage and challenge you to live fully and passionately. We'll discuss everything from setting priorities to managing PMS, from finding joy to taking care of yourself in the midst of all your responsibilities.

Don't close this book until you've shared your address with me. That way we can continue our dialogue!

Blessings,

Mary